SILETA HODGE

For Such A Time As This

Intimate Conversations, Divine Impartations,
Instant Deliverance

GET OVER HIM IN AN HOUR

Copyright © 2019, **Sileta Hodge**

The names and details of some of the stories mentioned herein have been altered to protect the privacy of individuals.

Book edited by: Dimikki Finley
Cover design: Sileta Hodge
Author Photo: Julian Reynolds

Published by Indigo Blu Publishing, 2019
Location: Atlanta, GA
Biblical References Included

ISBN: 9781791782078

Acknowledgements

First, I want to thank you God for placing this book within me and then giving me the grace to birth it. Writing it was quite a journey, but you took me through it. I am thankful to my family for their support. To Celeste, Aisha, Peta, Alfa, Kishma, and Rock Star, you guys rock! *Reggie*, I have always told you that if ever there was a past life, I have loved you in it, I love you now, and I plan to love you forever. *You are my rock*. To all my sisters around the globe: *Get well. And do it soon*. We've got work to do!

Table of Contents

GET OVER HIM IN AN HOUR

Preface

WE HAVE TO ADMIT IT WOMEN: We really do a lot of stupid things to mess our lives up. Psychotherapist, Dr. Laura Schlessinger, wrote an entire book about this in 1994, and it remains a timeless piece of work because women have continued to make choices that adversely affect them in the present and long run. We marry men who we know are not capable of loving us. We have continued to bring children into this world—whether inside or outside of a marriage—and are doing so with partners who are not committed to us, yet we expect them to commit to and be active in the lives of our children. We have continued to foolishly forgive and stay with adulterous men and are then grieved when a routine check-up at the doctor's office returns positive for sexually-transmitted diseases. We create homes for insensitive, out of control, and even violent men, who in mere seconds and sometimes with words alone, tear us down. And if all of the above is not a slap in our own faces, when we are asked why we do these things, we often cough up this excuse—*Because I love him.*

I didn't write this book to tear down any of my fellow women. Nor did I write it to paint a bad picture of men. I wrote it because at one point in my life, I had to come to terms with the fact that I needed to accept responsibility for some of the crosses I had welcomed and even nurtured in my life. I welcomed a man's obsessive behavior and ignored all the red flags that said—run! He went from being obsessive and controlling, to privately abusive, and then publicly humiliating. And is if that wasn't enough, instead of walking away from him, I ran down the aisle and married the man.

It doesn't take a psychotherapist to confirm that I was broken way before entering into that relationship, because had I not been, I would've nipped it in the bud when the first warning signs started manifesting. When I look back at that dark and low point in my life, I am thankful that God loved me enough to reach into my mess, he looked beyond all the bad choices I had made against his will, and he pulled me out of it.

Do you realize how precious you are? How powerful you are? How much purpose is in you? When you realize that, you begin to live your life with a sense of urgency. You begin to pick up the pace. You don't entertain just any type of relationship or even friendship. You become more protective of your life and you start to treat relationships, marriages, and any type of commitment for that matter, as institutions that have the power to impact your life, and the lives of your children and their children, for generations to come.

If I had stayed in that hostile environment, this book wouldn't be in your hands today. In the same breath, if I hadn't gone through all of the trauma in the first place, this wouldn't be my story to tell. But because it is my story and the story of millions of women around this world who have been hushed into silence—whether it's because of shame, guilt, or fear, I want to use it as a healing tool. Laurell K. Hamilton, an American writer, said something that resonates with me today because of some of my own experiences. She said, "There are wounds that never show on the body that are deeper and more hurtful than anything that bleeds." Before we move into the first chapter, I want to ask you, *what type of wounds are you walking around with, that only you can see and only you can feel?*

I have read books that were written for women whose marriages were in trouble and even books that were written to teach women how to become better wives or how to keep a man. What I hadn't found however, was the book I needed when I was trapped in the wrong relationship and needed to find the right words or a forceful enough push to give me the strength to get out. I decided to write it myself.

When I first started writing this book, I didn't have a clue about the direction I was going with it. In fact, it wasn't until I completed it, that I asked God for his permission to release it. I really should've asked him for instructions before writing, because I ended up having to re-write the entire book!

It was through prayer and fasting that he gave me instructions on what to write, one chapter at a time. I didn't want to talk about any of my personal experiences or about my brush with domestic violence. Still, there was a heaviness on my fingers to write about some of it. For those of you who have suffered through emotional, mental, and even physical trauma, you need to know that there is healing in your story. Writing this book has healed me from pain, guilt, unforgiveness, and other things I hadn't realized were buried within me. While I was writing, God revealed to me that through this book, he would heal eight types of sufferings that too many of his daughters are experiencing today.

I don't have a ten-step process to offer you and I don't have a fix-it-all solution that will resolve your problems in an hour either. I have written personal letters to each of you in the beginning of each chapter to let you know that your tears haven't gone unnoticed and your pain hasn't gone unfelt. Some of you will find that more than one or all of these letters belong to you.

If, after reading this book, I can get you to consider that your healing starts with realizing that you are faced with a major problem to begin with; If I can get you to place value on your life and to consider that your days here on earth are numbered. If I can get you to build up just a little more emotional strength to make better decisions on who you let into your life and your children's lives, then I would know that I have done my job. In this hour, let your healing begin.

PART one

A War is Waging

INTRODUCTION

IT IS AROUND 3:30 IN THE MORNING. There is nothing but stillness and quietness in the room with me. I am peering through the darkness to settle my eyes on a small light in the ceiling. I am not afraid of the dark, though moments ago, something was in the room with me. I had a weird out of body experience too. I saw myself sitting on the bed with my back pressed against the wall. I was not able to see the perpetrator's face, but a force was fighting me, and I was fighting back with my mouth. I raised my voice high, as these words shot out, one right after the other: *"No weapon formed against me shall prosper! No weapon formed against me shall prosper! No weapon formed against me shall prosper!"*

I don't know if anyone else heard me, but each word I released was a victory. The attacker became annoyed and even more aggressive. It tried to shut me up but was unable to close my mouth. It then tried to reach for my tongue.

I kept repeating the words, *"No weapon formed against me shall prosper,"* until it finally released me.

It wasn't a man that had just attacked me. It was a demonic spirit. It waited until I had fallen asleep, and literally in the same hour, it attacked. I saw something in the spirit though. It was reaching for my tongue for a reason. This demon had an assignment. It wanted to silence me. I had said too much.

This book was not conceived by mistake. It is no co-incidence that the enemy came in to attack just two days before its release. It is no co-incidence that I have tried to release this book at least five times before, and it just didn't happen. Hours before the attack, I took the time to read through the entire manuscript one final time. When I got to the final page, I was able to see something I had never seen before. I saw the big picture. Finally, I was able to understand what God was doing. This book isn't just a declaration of freedom for women who are bound by un-Godly relationships. It is a clarion call to women around the globe to draw nearer to God so that they may abide in his love and grace.

I want you to know that just because you have picked up this book, the enemy is upset. Why? Because he knows that there is healing in it, he knows it is chain-breaking, and he knows that it will shred the blind folds from around a lot of eyes and take readers into a deeper spiritual experience with the Most-High. From the pages of this book,

4

thousands of stories will emerge, lives will be restored, and the grounds will shake under the feet of women who will begin marching towards their destiny.

So why **Get Over Him in an** Hour, you may ask? God's word says in 1 Peter 5:10 (KJV): "But the God of all grace, who hath called us unto his eternal glory by Christ Jesus, after that ye have suffered a while, make you perfect, stablish, strengthen, settle you."

The peculiar thing about that scripture is that God doesn't say what a while is. I'm sure you can agree though, that you have suffered long enough. That is why the mandate has been sent forth, that all of His daughters be released in this very hour. He wants to deliver you. As you are reading this book and making your declarations, you will find yourself drawing nearer and nearer to the presence of God. You will find that it is easier for you to release what you've been holding on to, because just like that demon who tried to silence me earlier, the enemy will have no choice but to let go of his grip on your life. *Say amen!*

To the woman who lost it suddenly:

Dear Woman of God,

It is sad that we share so many pains in common; still, our experiences are so different. The fact that you have come to the end of this road can only mean that God is about to set you on a new path. It is along that path that you will find your restoration. As you press your thumb against the spine of this book or trace your index finger across the surface of your device, I pray that the words herein come alive and minister to that area in your life where you've been abandoned, where your hope has dried up, and where your patience has run thin.

You've prayed about it. You've cried about it. You've lost your mind because of it, and now it is time for you to release it. I pray that God grants you the serenity to accept the things you cannot change, the courage to change the things you can, and the wisdom to know the difference. He wants to restore you. He wants to heal you. He wants to catapult you into a new season, but you must first let go of what has already let go of you. You are no longer trapped for God has opened the door for you to get out of that poison situation that has kept you tied up and that has stagnated you. If

7

this book has landed in your hands and you know for a fact that you are in a relationship that God has not approved or led you to, then you should know that this is your Grace period. The Red Sea has parted, and God has made a way for you to get out, but time is of the essence.

Not another week. Not another day. Not another hour. The time for your deliverance is now. As you turn these pages, I pray that you are reminded of the brevity of life so that you may gain wisdom. We are all here on assignment and time wasted with the wrong person can cause us to miss our purpose—our mission—our destiny. In this hour, may the pain that has been consuming your life, dissipate.

You may feel lost and without direction, but really, you are right where you need to be. Sometimes God's timing can be abrupt, but when he is ready to move in your life, he removes all of the obstacles that are in the way. Sometimes to do this, he has to remove the blindfolds from around your eyes so that he can reveal to you who is who among you. You may feel as though you are losing your mind and you may feel lost and confused. This is exactly why the first chapter

8

was dedicated to you. Your pain is unique, especially since you lost it the way you did. It is also unique because of the pain you have endured and the shame you have experienced.

Because of your suffering, you are entitled to complete restoration and you are entitled to it in this season. In Joel 2:25 he promises that he will restore the years that the locust hath eaten, and the caterpillar, and the palmerworm, and the cankerworm. If I were you, I would replace my weeping with shouts and praises because what's coming to you is greater than what you have lost.

God's love and speed be with you.

CHAPTER

1

YOU ARE Being Re-Routed

FOR A SHORT TIME, while I lived in Florida, I attended a small Holy-Ghost filled church where the pastor and prayer warriors constantly preached and fought against *spiritual wickedness* in *high and low* places. Later on, along my spiritual journey, I gained a better understanding of just how serious the spiritual world is. I realized that the "enemy" was working full-time to hi-jack my mind, to steal my sanity, and most of all, the enemy was in pursuit of my life. In realizing how much I was under attack then and how little I understood about the spiritual world, I am amazed by God's grace and mercy towards me. He didn't allow the enemy's plan for my life to succeed. I understand too, that the prayers of my mother, the church warriors, the little utterances from my own mouth—the interplay of all three, kept my head above water. When death showed up for justice for my iniquities and disobedient spirit, mercy slammed its hand against the table and said *No—not my daughter*!

I think back to an early January morning; the sun hadn't come out yet and the dew had already started settling on blades of grass outdoor. I sat quietly on my balcony after my husband then, agreed with me that we had journeyed to the end of our marriage. While he was in the bedroom packing every piece of clothing that he owned, something inside of me wanted to say*, No. Don't Go. Stay.* But I knew that the grace I was granted for that relationship was running thin. The walls in my living room told stories of their own; a hole here, a dent there, shattered glass on the floor, some on the carpet. Above the couch, scripted imprints of words that held truth, whether good or bad. The words read: *We will always have these memories to share.*

He left quietly, like a disheartened crowd leaving a theatre after a sad movie. But our relationship was no movie. An hour before, I had been standing face to face with the devil. Alcohol lacing his breath, not a glint of love in his eyes. It was my first time seeing him after he had disappeared for months. I used to fight with the devil inside of him too. I would become enraged, throwing my voice around the room, waking the neighbors and their children. I couldn't stomach the woman I was becoming. I watched the love fade from my own eyes as bitterness and regret slowly filled my heart.

I wish I knew then, what I know now: I was fighting in the flesh against something that was attacking me in the spirit. Ephesians 6:12 (KJV) teaches: "For we wrestle not against flesh and blood, but against principalities, against powers, against rulers of the darkness of this world, against spiritual wickedness in high places."

I had stepped out of God's will and married this man, when deep down, I knew that I was making the wrong decision. Even on my wedding day, my spirit was troubled. A voice within me let me know that I would suffer the consequences of this choice I was making. I knew my husband had a drinking problem, but I figured that for the sake of our marriage, he would put down the bottle and take the necessary steps towards getting his life in order. I also knew that I wasn't ready to be a wife and that there were a lot of strong holds that God had to break off of me as well. My quick temper was one of them. The marrying of his addiction and my bad temper was a poison recipe that we both drank together.

I will never forget the prayers that I sent up to heaven one night while I was making my way home from a tiring shift I had completed at the law firm I was working at. I was pushing my way through heavy rainfall, and while I was driving, I cried out to God and asked him for deliverance. The more I was trying to make my marriage work, the more it was falling apart. I didn't even recognize myself nor the stranger in my home anymore. We were two strange people, fighting to live with the decisions we had made. When I had done all I knew to do, I finally asked God to just have his way.

I don't believe in co-incidences. I don't believe you picked this book up by mistake. Whatever the situation you are faced with, it is time to stop allowing it to take away your peace. I've always believed that who is supposed to be in our lives, will stay in our lives. And who is supposed to leave, by divine order, they have no choice but to go. We are all special in God's eyes, though I firmly believe that some of us are set apart, and therefore chastened by him. God is a God of restoration. He is a God of order. He is always on time. When you ask for deliverance, he will show up, and he will do so on his time. He wants us to walk in his will, he wants us to seek him out for guidance, but he also gives us the free will to make decisions for ourselves. When you're faced with a situation where you don't know if you should stay or go, always say, *God—have your way*!

God Have Your Way!

When you ask God to have his way, he has his way; and don't be surprised if he does it immediately. Once I surrendered, he started shifting things around in my life. At that time, I was working two full-time jobs, all while completing my bachelor's degree. It was so overwhelming, I became a robot, not really thinking, just doing what I felt programmed to do. Some mornings, I didn't have the desire or strength to get dressed or to even comb my hair. Even robots will power down when they don't have regular maintenance.

The day after I cried out to God on the highway, I went about my regular routine: coffee, a mumbled prayer, and a faint enough smile not to draw too much attention to my reality. I wrapped things up at my day job and with only thirty minutes to make it to the law firm that I worked at in the evenings, I quickly clocked out and brushed past my co-workers. I needed to beat the 5 p.m. traffic. I wouldn't make it to my car before my phone started ringing, however. It was one of the managers at the law firm. The voice on the other end of the line expressed deep regrets before asking me not to come in for my regular shift and not to come in again. I didn't ask why. The day I took the job, God had informed me that my time there would not exceed six months. Even though I had plans of staying longer, God made it clear that he had other plans for me. He released me from that job, exactly on the last day of the sixth month. As you are reading this book, I want to ask you to grab a notebook or a sheet of paper and write this down: *God has other plans for me.*

A Woman's Intuition

I didn't go straight home that evening. Instead, I sat quietly in a coffee shop, watching as customers strolled in and out, some taking seat next to me. I wondered about their lives, whether they were single, dating, happily married, or divorced. One couple who appeared to be married, was playfully flirting with each other as they were standing in line. Then at one end of the store, I caught a glance at a gay couple who were proudly holding hands. I asked myself if anything could be done at all to fix my own relationship. My marriage had become so bitter, my husband and I were strangers in our own home. Right where I was seated, God began to speak to me and he started removing the wool from around my eyes so that he could show me where I was and what it was that I was trying to save.

You may be reading this book right now and maybe you have been praying desperately for God to fix your relationship. *God can fix anything.* Sometimes though, the things we are asking him to fix, are the exact same things that he is asking us to walk away from.

There was so much anger and bitterness built up in me, so much healing that I needed, not just because of the relationship, but healing from things I hadn't dealt with before entering into that marriage. Those things had piled up, one thing on the other, and had started to fester inside of me. God was saying to me that it was time to heal. Night came down on me while I was still sitting inside of that coffee shop. Right when I was about to leave, I had a strange gut feeling that prompted me to pull open my laptop and to start doing some research.

The first thing I thought I needed to access was my husband's personal bank account. Now, before you get to judging me, this was something I never did before or ever thought I had a reason to do. We have personal accounts for a reason, after all. But I couldn't understand why I felt a heaviness to do that right then and there. More shocking was the fact that I managed to guess his username and

17

password. I was looking left and right and over my shoulder to make sure no one saw what I was doing. Yes! I felt guilty. But I lowered that screen anyways and the first thing that caught my eyes was a charge that was made to his account that day. It was for a night's stay at a nearby hotel. I never in a million years would've suspected my husband of cheating. He was a drunk and he was abusive. But cheating? *No—not him.*

I looked up the information to the hotel. I couldn't just stop there either. I needed to know more. I called the front desk, and without thinking of what I was going to say, I quickly explained that I had just dropped a man and a woman off. I provided his name and told her he had left medication in my car and that I needed to speak to him right away. Sounds urgent enough, right? *Of course, I was lying.* God forgive me. But my heart skipped a few beats when she asked me to hold. She transferred me to his room. When he picked up, my heart stopped beating. It was true. He had booked a hotel room. He was with another woman.

"Everything makes sense now," I said to him. All I could hear was breathing on the other end of the line. He didn't say a word to me. He didn't come home that night. And for nearly two months, he was neither seen nor heard from. When he finally showed up, the devil decided to turn that visit into a war.

Isn't it amazing how a woman's intuition works though? We usually know what we think we know. God allowed me to see this so that he could reveal to me that what I was holding on to had left the building a long time ago. My husband had moved on. It was now time for me to move on.

The night he moved out, the hardest rainfall I'd ever seen or heard, poured down in my city. I didn't have an appetite to eat, and I kept my phone on do not disturb so not to be bothered by friends or family. I sat in my favorite place, on the balcony, looking out at the rain drops as they sent ripples across the lake. A strange feeling started welling up inside of me. It was a feeling of defeat and of rejection. Words that were spoken against me years ago started sounding in my ears. Words that said I was never going to amount to anything. Words that said I would never stay married or have a stable life. I felt like the enemy had been standing at the edge of the lake and was looking up at me with his arms folded, nodding his head and saying, "I won."

You who are reading this book right now, if this is how you feel, I want you to write on the same sheet of paper that you took out, "I am exactly where God needs me to be."

For you to understand the next leg of this chapter, you will need to open your spiritual eyes a bit, because I need you to understand what is about to happen next in your life. It is something that happens only in your surrender. While the enemy might have won the battle, he hasn't won the entire war. Yes, I said war, because the real war that the enemy is waging, is a war over your life. This is why suicide is considered a global public health concern in the world today. Even though suicide rates are higher for men than they are for women, women make twice the number of suicide attempts as do men, it is just that these attempts are half the time unsuccessful. Researchers today are still trying to understand the relationship between gender and suicide. This is not the time to lose your mind, woman of God. Not at this junction in your life, where you are about to turn a new corner and do exploits. We are told in Ephesians 6:11, to put on the full armor of God, so that we can take our stand against the devil's schemes. In the next verse it tells us that we wrestle not against flesh and blood, but against principalities, against powers, against the rulers of the darkness in this world, against spiritual wickedness in high and low places.

The Armor of God

Now that you know what you are up against, it is important that you know what the full armor of God is, so that you can be prepared in this next season of your life. The six pieces of his armor include: The Belt of Truth, A Breastplate of Righteousness, Your Feet, The Shield of Faith, God's Salvation as your Helmet, and the Spirit as your Sword. We are asked to stand strong with the belt of truth fastened around our waist. The breastplate of righteousness has to do with living in pursuit of God. He tells us to wear the good news of peace on our feet so that we may be able to stand strong. This way, in each step that we take, we would be able to do so in full confidence. The shield of faith is what we use to stop the burning arrows that are aimed at us. His salvation is our helmet, which is important to understand, as your helmet is the covering you need, to keep you safe from the impact. Finally, the spirit is your sword. This has to do with the teachings of God. When you realize how armed you are in Christ, you will be more encouraged to draw closer to God so that you can fight the good fight of faith.

Pick up the Pace

My husband had disappeared, but to my surprise, a blanket of peace had fallen over me. This doesn't mean that an emotional war didn't ensue. But for a few days, I found peace. The house was the quietest it had ever been. I was able to rest. I was able to hear and listen to the voice within me. One day at a time, I was drawing closer to God. I was spending more time in his word. He started revealing bits and pieces of his plan for the next chapter of my life. I came into a period of surprises and rapid changes. Things were happening so quickly, I was forced to pick up the pace.

Before I could complete my college degree, I secured a management position with a company near my home. There was a desire within me to start my own business as well, but I had been going through so much and juggling so many different things at once, I couldn't pursue it like I wanted to. Not while I was attached to someone who was destroying all the good in me, anyway. For some reason though, I started getting a lot of calls and request for my services. I hadn't been working at the new firm for more than six months, before I realized that I would have to choose between working that job or jumping into business for myself. God didn't stop there either. He was speaking to me in the spirit, and one of the things he was asking me to do was to leave the new job, leave the city of Ft. Lauderdale, and head to Atlanta.

I strongly believe that a lot of women who identify with this chapter are in the same place today, as I was then. You are in a new season. You are being re-routed. Some of you reading right now have already been moved or directed to a new city, state, or even country. You have been set on an entirely new path. It may feel as though your life is falling apart but when the smoke clears, you will realize that what's really happening is that a significant part of your destiny has been activated, and some people do not have the clearance to journey with you, into that chapter of your life.

While I was busy picking up the pieces of my life, my husband went his way. He started his life with someone new. A month after our divorce, he was married again. *Can you believe that?* God was working on me though. He was polishing me. I faith-ed my way to Atlanta with my entire life crammed into a small Nissan Sentra. My car broke down along the way. It was easier to turn around and take it as a sign that I should not be going. I prayed over that car and pushed forward anyway, because I knew that my instructions were clear— *Go to Atlanta*! Write on that piece of paper: *I am going to push forward anyway.*

In this season of your life, you will be given specific instructions. Some of you have already received those instructions but you're afraid to do what you need to do. Whether that means walking away from the house, agreeing to partial custody of the children, renting an apartment across town, whatever it is, you need to stop doubting those instructions and make those changes. I followed God's directions without knowing what was in store for me. I followed him without knowing whether or not I was capable of running a business efficiently so that I can provide for myself. I followed him, and there were days when I didn't hear his voice at all. Days when he closed his mouth and maintained his silence. I wanted to know what was next. When you get to this point, my advice to you is to Keep Trusting God.

You lost it all and you lost it suddenly. I want to tell you though, that you might be crying over the illusion of something you think you had in the first place. I thought I had a great relationship. I thought I had something that was worth saving. I was thinking that way because that is the story I was telling myself, my friends, and my family. Over time, I started believing it.

The real story though is that I was running out of makeup to cover bruises from hands that were constantly being laid on me. I was covering wounds instead of getting down to the root of the problem. There were frequent visits to my home from police officers—calls I made because I wasn't sure how far things would go. I was losing sleep. I was sleeping with the enemy. The enemy was sleeping with other people.

If this is you, I am warning you—let go of the delusion that everything is perfect so that you may have room to take on real, fulfilling, and worthwhile experiences through people who are divinely tied to your destiny. The reason it all came crumbling down suddenly is because you have an appointment with destiny and God is re-routing you so that you can get back on track. Don't continue to allow your life, your blessings, and your entire future to be placed on hold, all because you are hanging on to the coat tail of a man who is not interested in building a life and a future with you.

When the smoke clears, we really start to see things for what they truly are. I was insecure with myself and I was in a low place spiritually. My husband couldn't love me because he hadn't first learned to love himself. I hadn't realized then that I had a purpose on this earth and that God had called me to be more than someone's punching bag.

When I stopped pretending like I had it all together, when I decided to surrender and ask God for his direction, when I decided to put God first, he stepped in and started working on me. He started healing me. He started grooming me for what was next. He began catapulting me into a new level in my life that I could not have dreamed for or anticipated. I had to trust him every step of the way.

He's going to do the same for you. But I want you to ask yourself this one question:

Is what I am crying over and holding on to worth missing out on the best days of my life, which are yet ahead of me?

To the woman stuck in a cycle

Dear Woman of God,

You may have asked yourself this question more than once in the past month or two: Why do I keep finding myself in the same situation—over and over? You get close to exhaling, you let your guards down, you tell yourself that this is your last stop, and then it all falls apart. I have been in this position, but there was a turning point in my life where I made up my mind that I was going to do something different so that I could get different results. In the discovery process of trying to understand why I was constantly being dragged into the same vicious cycle, I had to admit to a number of things: One, I was attracted to a certain type of man. Two, I had issues with "self" that I was deliberately suspending into the future. Three, I was not in the driver's seat of my destiny. I'll explain this third point a little further.

When you are in the driver's seat of your destiny, you know exactly what you want and therefore, you recognize what you don't want. This means that there are some things that you just won't put up with, like a man who doesn't come home every night, a man who won't commit, a man who sleeps around with other women, or a man who won't give you the title as his woman. Not only that, but when you aren't in the driver's seat of your destiny, you let the other person dictate a lot of your future. You'll know that this applies to you when you respond "Yes" to having said one of the following statements recently: "I'm just going to see what he's going to do and then I'll decide what I'm going to do" or, "If he doesn't do this, I'll just have to do that" and perhaps you've said this too, "I wish he would make up his mind and stop holding up my life." All of these statements suggest that your next move depends on his next move. Can you really afford to suspend your life in this way—especially for a man that you know is not tied to your destiny?

I strongly believe that there are aspects of our lives that we as women, simply cannot afford to make a compromise with. These things include our calling or higher purpose, our identity, and our destiny. But where cycle is concerned, I need you to understand this: One of the reasons you are stuck in the same vicious cycles is because you haven't put your foot down and decided to take control of your life and you haven't taken the time to discover who you are and what fabric you are cut from.

Your unique suffering is that you can't seem to make the right decisions for yourself. You can't seem to break away from your bad choices of men. You can't seem to break away from un Godly soul ties, you can't seem to break the strongholds, you can't seem to face your own insecurities to realize why you keep settling.

The scripture teaches that we are destroyed for lack of knowledge (Hosea 4:6). How much do you know about yourself? When was the last time you stopped to analyze your behavior? What spirits do you need to defeat so that you can free yourself of the cycle that you are trapped in? It is hard to win a war, when you do not know the enemy you are up against.

While writing this chapter, I struggled with deciding how much I wanted to share with you. I shared what God asked me to share and I held back the rest. From the spiritual attacks, the spiritual husbands, to repeating the same mistakes, and then finally seeking help and taking control of my life. I can honestly say I am now in control of my destiny—of course, with God leading the way.

By the end of this chapter, I trust that you too will be released and set free to live the life that God intended you to live. You will become a new woman, one who knows what she wants out of life, one who respects herself, and one whose steps are ordered by God. As much as I struggled with this chapter, I rejoiced, because I knew that from it, a stampede of women would come forth, and you my friend, are a part of that march. Can you feel the ground trembling beneath you as you take your first steps forward?

Your healing starts in this hour!

CHAPTER

2

UNBROKEN Cycles

WE MAY NOT ALL ADMIT IT, but most of us are carrying open wounds from the violent lacerations we received in the spiritual, verbal, and or physical battles we have encountered through men who should have loved, cherished, and protected us. Some of whom, even in their absence, have managed to kill parts of us. Too many of us have wounds that have been left out in the open, have been left unattended to, untreated, and unaddressed. Should these wounds go ignored another month, another week, another hour, I am afraid that a handful of us will slip further into vicious cycles of unforgiveness, mistrust, and perpetual abuse.

The summer before I completed this book, I was conducting a mentoring session downtown Atlanta with a new client who was excited about starting up a non-profit. I was thrilled to learn that the programs in her organization were designed to help women who were affected by domestic partner violence, specifically those who were critically injured and facing homelessness. I listened very closely as she spoke, and by the inflections in her voice, it was easy to tell that this was an organization she had spent a lot of time planning for. She knew what her target market looked like, she had assessed the community and knew that Georgia was placed among the top fifteen in the nation for deaths resulting from domestic violence. She also realized that no matter what services she offered, it would be up to these women to make the decisions for themselves to break out of the cycles that they had caught themselves in.

As she continued speaking about the programs, I noticed that her voice grew more and more shaky, until finally she suddenly burst out into tears. I couldn't imagine that she was crying for the women she hadn't even met yet. I knew immediately that the tears were falling from a personal place inside of her. A place where a war went down and parts of her had died. She had a story that needed to be told. If you still have your pen and paper out, I want you to write down: *I too, have a story that needs to be told.*

I didn't want to interrupt her or to seem insensitive, but I needed to know her story, so naturally, I asked her what was going on. I fought back my own tears as she pointed to parts of her face where her child's father, had twenty years ago, used a razor to cut into her skin, even tearing into the sides of her mouth and between her eyebrows.

"He was aiming for my throat," she explained, swallowing hard, as if it the razor was stuck in there somewhere. She looked off to the side before talking again. "It was by the grace of God that I got away with my life."

When I asked her how exactly she got away, she patted her tears with a napkin I had handed to her, and gathered herself together, before explaining that it was a decision she had to make for both she and her son. She was in her early twenties at that time, and she knew that this relationship held no promises of life for either of them. She took her son, the little money she had in her account, and only a few of their belongings, before taking a long journey from New York City to Atlanta.

Later that afternoon, as I made my way from the downtown office I mentored out of, I wondered about the women I passed on the sidewalk. What were their stories? What types of open wounds were they carrying? What types of scars were hidden under their makeup?

That entire week, the look of terror on that woman's face stayed with me. How did something that had happened over two decades ago still have the power to haunt her through a mere recollection of the event?

There was something she said before she left, that stuck with me too. She said to me, *Sileta, I want to help all women, but mainly those who don't know better. Some of them have chosen to stay in the cycles that they are in, and when they make that choice, not much can be done to help them.* I wanted to refute her statement. I wanted to point out to her that women who end up in these situations are helpless and they don't know better. I wanted to defend us. I wanted to tell her that after what she herself had been through, the audacity of her to say something like that. The more I tried to find reasoning to back my position, the more I realized that a lot of us, including myself in the past, have foolishly played Russian Roulette with our lives. One of the reasons we have done this is because it is hard to see the picture when we are the ones in the frame. And we often don't realize how much danger we are in. *I get it.* A lot of this is because of the brainwashing that we have come under. So we stick around, at the risk of our very own lives. And too often, the very safety of our children's lives, is placed at risk too.

If we look at Erik Erikson's stages of psychosocial development, we will learn that an infant of roughly 0 to 18 months goes through the psychosocial crisis of Trust vs. Mistrust. In that time, the infant learns certain patterns concerning the care they are receiving. As long as that care is consistent, predictable, and reliable, the child feels a sense of security, and they also learn to trust. On the contrary, however, if the care they are receiving is harsh and unpredictable, they begin to develop mistrust. Which ever of the two the infant develops in this stage, Erikson theorized that they will carry it with them into other relationships. The only predictor the child has that would allow it to determine whether to trust or distrust is *consistency*. The child analyzes the patterns of its caretakers and from this, begins to make predictions of future behavior. You may be wondering, *where exactly is Sileta going with this?*

I use this theory to highlight the parallels between the intelligence of an infant and its ability to pick up patterns in order to make a judgment on who can and cannot be trusted; and then, our innate ability as women to recognize patterns of behavior in the men we choose to give ourselves to. I point this out to highlight the fact that we are, indeed, smarter than some of the decisions we have made in the past. Once we are clear on that, we have eliminated the excuses that often slip through our mouths on why we didn't know better, how we were fooled, and why we feel sorry for ourselves. It is really time to stop with the excuses, admit that we knew better, and even when we really didn't know better, to at least learn from our mistakes. I am not blaming you for what happened. I am simply saying, it is your responsibility to get out of it.

Outside of Erikson's theory, studies in neuroscience have proven that the essence of the evolved human brain is superior pattern processing (SPP), which among other factors, is directly linked to human intelligence, our ability to be creative, our capacity to learn language, and even our ability to make decisions. Both religion and science confirm that we as humans, are innately intelligent, and any deviance from this is suggestive of some type of malfunction. Scientists believe that a broader understanding of SPP mechanisms and the role they assume in both the normal and abnormal function of the human brain, may one day allow for the development of interventions that reduce the irrational decisions that we make. But do we really need neuroscience to step in and tell us that we need to make better choices when it comes to choosing a mate?

The ultimate freedom that anyone can have when it comes to love is being able to take control of the type of relationship(s) they are participating in and saying no to everything that doesn't look like it, doesn't sound like it, doesn't smell like it, doesn't taste like it, and doesn't feel like it. Love is a choice. If I can get you to agree on this with me, you are already on your way to breaking the unhealthy patterns of thought that have been influencing the decisions you have been making. Don't beat yourself up for the bad choices you've made in the past. The very fact that you are reading this book suggests that you want to make a change. Good for you. Now let's go deeper into cycles.

Recognizing Vicious Cycles

I did a brief study on the etymology of the word "cycle" and came across a 14th century definition that stemmed from the old French derivative "Cicle". In that definition, it was explained that a cycle is a "Perpetual circulating period of time, on the completion of which certain phenomena return in the same order." During that time, the word was used by the French, and in different versions, by the Latin, and the Greek to explain astronomical phenomena that was happening in our universe.

I considered the cycles that I have encountered in my own universe or personal world, whether it was a cycle of allowing people who continually hurt me, to come back into my life; or more common, attracting the same type of male into my life—over and over. A lot of times, these were aggressive men, men with "situation-ships", men who were not looking to settle down, men with "mommy" issues, men with "daddy" issues, men who were still "boys", men who weren't into me like "that", and so on. After hearing the same lines, witnessing the same schemes, and reaping the same rotten fruits of my investments in these types of commitments, I realized that something inside of me needed to change. I needed what was attracted to me and what I was attracted to, to shift. I soon realized that the thing that needed to change was my level of maturity and my mindset.

We are scripturally taught that we are transformed by the renewing of our minds (Romas12:2). When we make this change, we come to know God's will for us and that which is pleasing in his sight. He gives us discernment so that we may be able to see in people, beyond what our physical eyes can perceive. This is exactly why, when we

38

meet certain people, we get a vibe or a feeling about them. We usually pick this up when we first come into contact with them. But often times we shove this knowledge aside, because we are attracted to something in the physical realm, and this doesn't always have to be looks either, because let's admit it women—even the most *unattractive* of men have done us some unimaginable harm. Seriously, I can't tell how many of my girlfriends I have sat over wine with as they were going through a heart break, and in the middle of sobbing, watched them burst out into laughter before admitting things about the man's features that they couldn't believe they had settled for—whether it was a beer belly, a beard that didn't connect, or feet that did not need to be exposed in the open at any point—ever; meanwhile, these men had succeeded in making them feel unattractive, unpretty, or inferior at some point. But this discussion is in no way about what we have settled for. Instead, I want to point out where these cycles begin.

They start the very moment we ignore our spirit, or some may call it *the gut feeling*. When we ignore this and override it with our emotions, we often find ourselves in big trouble. As women, we have a powerful gift that no man on earth can deny us—that is our intuition. It tells us when something is wrong. It warns us when we are in danger. It helps us to pick up on a shift in something that was once routine. Even with this gift—we too often ignore our inner GPS when it begins alarming and saying, *Make a U-turn! Make a U-Turn! Make a U-turn!* Some of us ignore this GPS for months and years, and then wonder why we end up deserted and on empty further down the road.

I Changed My Mind

I told you in the first chapter that I changed states. What I didn't tell you is that I honestly hadn't really changed my mind. Because of that, I was still attracting the same type of demons into my life. I will explain further, but first let's look at the etymology of the word *catapult*. I used it in the previous chapter and I am going to refer back to it several times in this book. The Latin version of the word which is "Catapulta" means "war machine for throwing". When God placed his hand into time and pulled me out of an abusive relationship, he then catapulted me to a place that was designed for my healing. He gave me an entirely new life and a fresh start. But I reverted back to the same mindset, the same impaired way of thinking, and because of this, I attracted the same type of man into my life.

It was an older man this time. I couldn't believe I was opening up my heart to someone so soon. We dated for some time. I remember the butterflies that would spring up in my stomach whenever I saw him or whenever he called. It was good having him around. I admired how skilled he was with his hands, how hardworking he was, and the beautiful way he was patient with me. It didn't take long, however, for me to learn that I was entertaining the same spirt, just in a new person.

His true colors came out one night while we were hanging out at my apartment. My cell phone was ringing, and when I realized that it was an overseas number, I picked up. To my surprise, it was an old college classmate whom I hadn't heard from in ages. *The man*—who was now standing next to me, became outraged over what was a normal conversation with exchanges of "how-do-you-do's" "how's your career?" and "how's your family?" Before I could finish the conversation, the charming man I had almost fallen in love with, flipped my office desk over while I was still sitting there, sending my flowers, my laptop, and some of my files flying to the ground. I couldn't believe my eyes. There I was, in the confines of my own apartment, in a new state, away from anyone I knew, and standing in front of me was an enraged stranger—but far worst—a familiar spirit.

A Familiar Spirit

In the spirit world, I recognized what it was. The same demon had found me again. But how did it find me here? How did it find me in this new person? How did it manage to work its way in? I called the cops and asked him to leave. To say I was shaken up, would be an understatement.

I remember placing a phone call to his sister that night. She sat quietly on the other line and soaked up every word I was sharing with her. When I was done talking, she apologized to me. She explained that she could've told me that he was this way. She had only hoped that he had changed his ways, especially when she saw how happy he was, the day he introduced me to her. She went on to say that I hadn't seen half of what he was capable of.

"End whatever the two of you have going on, right now!" was her warning. She also let me know that she felt sorry for me, but that if I chose to move forward with him, she would not sit on the other end of the line and throw a pity party for me the next time. This was the only pity party I was ever going to have. Not even an hour after I spoke to her, a strange number was calling. When I picked up, it was his mother. She expressed how sorry she was, and then warned me to never speak to her son again. Just like his sister, she too thought he had changed.

It was clear he hadn't. Apparently, this man had a history of being abusive to the women in his life.

The Roll Over Rule

He called and explained that he was sorry. That he got a little jealous. That he would never do that again. I had heard that so many times before through the person before him, there was no way I was going to continue on in that same cycle. I call it *the roll-over rule*. Whatever you could no longer tolerate or had enough of in the previous relationship, do not let it roll over into the next. You served your time. If or when it shows up in the next person, do not put up with it. Not even for a second.

I took control of my life after that first episode and I made sure that it was the last. I was ashamed. I was embarrassed. I knew that God was upset with me, even though he had protected me. I was so serious about moving on, I leased a second apartment on the other side of town, not even a week later, and paid out the remaining months in the current lease. We never saw each other after that. Sometimes when we break the cycle though, we are left with the soul tie.

Ungodly Soul Ties

One of the quickest ways to unleash hell in your life is by way of an ungodly soul tie. These types of soul ties often extend beyond the actual relationship. This is why a lot of you cannot let go. The man has already moved on and you're still calling him. Still crying over him. Still trying to figure out what happened or where you went wrong.

Soul ties hinder your growth and impede on your ability to move on. Some of you have even met a decent and well-meaning man but are about to chase him away because you are conflicted by a soul tie. Many of you have more than one soul ties and because of this, you have been kept in a cycle of sleeping with the same men, over and over. You don't even understand why you're doing it. You don't even realize that in doing this, you are inviting demons into your life. Not only that, but you have lost so much of who you are, all because you have taken up bits of pieces of them, their bad habits, and their traits; you have even inherited some of the curses attached to them. This is why so many of you are being terrorized by spirits of depression, anxiety, suicide, confusion, hatred, unforgiveness, lack, bitterness, grief; I could go on and on.

If after reading this you realize that you have an un Godly soul tie, I want you to stop where you are, and I want you to begin praying and asking God to help you to sever those ties. Declare and decree that you will no longer be connected to anyone who is not tied to your destiny or who is not supposed to be tied to you in this season. Declare right now that this is the last day, last hour, last minute that you will be tied to this man, this entity, this being. Put this book down right now and start removing those chains in the spirit world. Start opening up your mouth and saying enough is enough. I can't stress enough how important it is for you to use your mouth to change the atmosphere around you. Some of you, your homes have gotten unusually cold, unusually uninhabitable, it has become a place that when you walk in, you can't rest. You can't sleep. When night falls, a blanket of depression falls over you. Your bed has become the most dreadful place to be in. That's because you have invited spirits in that you need to give an eviction notice to now! In fact, don't even give a notice. It is time to put them out. Use your mouth. Take your bible up. Get in God's word. Chase those devils out!

You will know that it is a soul tie when you can admit that this is not the man who God has for you, especially because of how he has treated you, yet you can't seem to stop thinking of him. Some of you have been beaten, humiliated, even spat at by these men, and are still hoping that they will have a change of heart, that they will call you back and make things right. You have spent months, and some of you, even years, holding on to a dead thing, when really, they shouldn't have even been given an hour of your time. If this is you, you have a soul tie and you need to cut it off.

You have to understand that the only way to entertain a soul tie is to step outside of your element and be something other than what you were called to be. When you are not walking on the path that you should be on, you begin to settle for a lower vibrating version of yourself. This version of yourself will entertain anything on its current level or lower and will run away from anything that vibrates higher. When you find yourself forcing a man to love you, or when you are constantly forcing a relationship to work, you are soul tied to that person. It is time you stop chasing after that man, get yourself together, and work at becoming a better version of you. You cannot force someone to love you. Soul ties are evidence that you have a lot of work to do on yourself. Just as bad as a soul tie, if not worse, is a spiritual husband. You need to break those off of you too.

Spiritual Husbands

I did not know that there was such a thing as a spiritual husband or even a spiritual wife, until I had a supernatural encounter while spending the night with a guy that I was dating. I had fallen asleep in his bed and while I was asleep, a woman placed her hands on my shoulder and woke me up. Well, she actually shook me up. Her name was Kathy. I'm not sure how I knew her name, but she came to me in the form of a dream. Kathy was marching in a line, next to hundreds of other women. I was standing off to the side, watching these women go by— almost in a forward robotic stride. That's when Kathy turned her head and looked me dead in the eyes. She was wearing a black dress, her face was a pale white, and her hair was silver. She left the line and walked towards me. Then when she got in reach, she placed her hands on my shoulder and started commanding, "Get up! Get up! Get up!"

I jumped up out of my sleep, but Kathy was still there. And, she was still holding me by the shoulder. I could feel her! Freaked all the way out, I jumped out of the bed, and tumbled over a basket of clothes, before flipping on the light switch. The commotion I made caused the guy to wake up. I imagine I looked like a crazy woman with wild eyes, as I was trying to search for Kathy in the ceiling, behind the doors, and under the bed. I was out of breath. My friend tried to calm me down, and when I was finally able to relax, I told him what had happened. He looked at me with some skepticism before laughing and telling me everything was okay and that I should come back to bed.

I was not going to chance hopping back into this man's bed though. *Nope. Not me.* I gathered my belongings and left. Kathy had spoken loud and clear. She had warned me. She was saving me from something and I was not going to learn the hard way, what that something was. Some of you have been ignoring the warning signs. You have elected to remain ignorant. You have become an enemy to yourself. When has your life become such a joke, that you don't have enough respect to walk away from something that no longer serves you?

Maybe a year after the ordeal, I ran into the same guy, and he invited me to lunch. It was over lunch that he confessed to me that he knew what had happened that night. He first started off by telling me that he couldn't believe that I was able to see in the spirit world, something that had been affecting him for most of his adult life. Mind you, up until that point, I still had no clue as to what had happened that night. But he went on to explain that there are two female spirits in his life that have been blocking him from having meaningful relationships. These spirits, he explained, were attached to him at a very young age, when he was introduced to various types of magic. The hair on my body stood up as he explained his past, his family history with what island people call— *obeah*, and I suppose witchcraft, and how these spirits have remained with him. Whoever Kathy was, I was thankful for the wake-up call. But do you see how important it is for us to be careful with whom we attach ourselves to?

I don't think I fully understood the term spiritual husband either, until I got more serious about my Christian walk and realized that there was a spiritual husband attached to my life as well. This spirit would visit me at nights, press me down in my sleep, and even attempt sexual activities with me. For some of you, this may sound new, and you may even be thinking, *this girl is crazy*. But these things I am sharing with you are all real. As you begin to search the internet, you will find hundreds, if not thousands of similar stories about these spirit visits, and how women and men have been violated by them.

Some of you reading this right now have a spiritual husband and perhaps even a spiritual wife attached to you. The mission of these spirits is to keep you single. To keep you in isolation. To prevent you from having the desire to have a meaningful relationship. Some of you have lost the desire to become a wife one day, or to have a family. You have been glorifying the idea of being single forever. Of course you can do bad all by yourself. But how about sharing your life experience with someone who God has designed just for you. Someone who understands you, who can put up with the parts of you that no one else appreciated. Some of you can't even get comfortable around the man you're with, because you've got to keep your makeup on, you've got to keep your wigs on, you've got to wear the best outfit. How about being yourself for a change? I bring these points up because I have been there and trust me, there is no real beauty like feeling like you're beautiful inside out. If someone can't accept you for who you are, cut them and their demons off, and keep it moving.

I get it. It is not easy to cut someone off, especially when you are soul-tied to them, especially when you depend on them to pay the bills, especially when your name is tied up in a two-year contract with the cable company that is addressed to their home, and especially when the family-plan phone contract is in your name or theirs. Some of you, you are the one who has been giving to this man. You pay his bills. He only pays you enough attention to take what he can get. And you're okay with this, just as long as he tells you he loves you. Just as long as he makes promises to you—even if he cannot keep them. I am telling you, it is time you get rid of these ties, these spirits, and this frame of thinking. These spirits aren't easily broken off of your life either. You will have to go into perpetual praying and fasting until they are completely eradicated. Do not play around with them. Do not entertain them. Rebuke them. Declare that your mind lines up with what God is calling you to in this season. Trust me sisters, it is time to get out of your current frame of mind. It is time to shatter the delusion. It is time to tap in to your superwoman strength, start opening your mouth, declaring the word of God over your life, and once and for all, bring those cycles to an end.

Cycles keep you in a state of roaming. When you're in roaming, it is hard for you to be fruitful when it comes to your relationships. That is why you keep going from one relationship to the next. These relationships don't advance, they don't mature, they don't grow. It is time for you to bear fruit. Put on the armor of God and start breaking those cycles. And while you're at it, break the generational curses too.

Generational Curses

A while back, while I was fasting, I got a revelation about generational curses, how they target the womb and pass on violently from one generation to the next. And how a lot of times, it is not a new spirit, but the same ugly spirit that is assigned to a family's lineage, that keeps causing major upheavals, and it disrupts the lives of certain family members, if not all. It sits there causing wreak and havoc until someone is bold enough to pull out a sword, slay those demons, and break that curse. It was through prayer, fasting, and spending time in the word that I learned too that God punishes even the children, for the sins of their fathers (Deuteronomy 5:9). It seems harsh, but when we think of it, if a child is exposed to a life where there is a perpetual abusing of drugs, where there is constant infidelity, where there is abuse, anger, mediocrity, stagnancy, and I could go on and on; this exposure increases the likelihood that the same behaviors will be picked up by the child.

Still, there are some instances where the child hasn't even been exposed to any of the above, maybe they were adopted, and for some reason, they behave in the same manner. They take up some of the same sins. No wonder the saying holds strong that the apple never really falls far from the tree. I wish I can just tell you that you can cancel a generational curse by repeating a few words, telling the devil to flee, and then poof, it will be gone. This is serious though. It will require a lot from you. The first step is finding evidence of that curse throughout your family. You have to realize that there is a problem. Some of you are not blind to it either. You can literally trace its footsteps from your great grandmother to you grandmother, down to your mother, and now you. I do believe that it skips some of us and goes to our children. The only way to break these curses is through heavy prayer, fasting, and through full repentance and salvation in Jesus Christ. Let's talk about this some more.

The Men in Your Life

Think about your father, your son, or that man you are trying to get over. What type of curses have they passed down to you or you them? Some of you may very well be fighting to be with someone who God is trying to steer you away from because of the curses attached to their lives. It is time women, that you survey the men in your lives, study them and identify their strengths and weaknesses, and then make a determination of the role you will play in their healing. If any at all.

Some of these men, the only way you will be able to help them to heal is with a hands-off approach. Yes ladies—you can pray for some of these men from a distance. You can forgive them and still move on. Now don't get me wrong. We all have things that we are fighting with. Things that we are struggling with. None of us are perfect. What I am trying to point out to you though, is this: *you don't have to settle*. You especially should not ignore "certain" character flaws when they manifest through the people you interact with. Here are some of the character flaws I think you should walk or even run away from when they manifest:

1. Someone who is not God-fearing
2. Someone with a short temper
3. Someone who is verbally abusive
4. Someone who is physically abusive
5. Someone with a lying tongue
6. Someone who will not commit
7. An alcoholic or someone who is abusing drugs
8. Someone who is willfully blind to their flaws
9. Someone who cannot be reasoned with
10. Someone who doesn't respect you
11. Someone who doesn't respect themselves
12. Someone who doesn't respect others
13. Someone who is dishonest with dealings

Also, while you're at it. Say NO to:

1. Baby Momma Drama
2. Momma's boy-syndrome
3. Can't ever find a job. Can't Keep a job
4. I'll drop you to work and do nothing all day. In Your car.
5. "Can I borrow, X amount from you?"

Nothing's wrong with being there for a man. But some of you need to practice being there for yourself and your children first. I don't know what the government is dropping in the water these days, but it seems to me that a lot of men have forgotten that they are naturally wired to be providers. This isn't to say that women shouldn't help out. We are designed to be help mates after all. Some women, including myself, are comfortable with being an equal mate. Really, the only time a woman should ever be taking care of a man financially is if that's her husband and that's something they agreed on, for whatever reason. Outside of that, you ain't got no business taking care of a grown man who was two working feet and hands but *does not want to go out there and work.*

I don't know about you, but it is a good feeling to have my own and to be independent. Yet, it is an even better feeling to know that my man can hold things down if for whatever reason, I can't. Again, I'm not saying don't be there for a man. I'm simply saying, help those who are really trying to help themselves. But I'm warning you also, to help yourself and your children first, especially if this is someone who is not committed to you. I would much rather help them as a friend and leave the relationship alone altogether, than to give them my hard-earned money, just to have them around.

For those of you who are raising sons, especially those doing it on your own, please instill in them at an early age, the importance of work ethic. I am not telling you to take the kid out of school and make them get a job. You can teach a child work ethic by offering lessons bout discipline. Simple things like waking up at a certain time or going to bed at a certain time. Teach them how to be responsible. Teach them the importance of order. Instill biblical principles in your children at an early age. It is not the world's responsibility to teach them. But if you don't teach them—the world will. And when the world does, you risk the chance of them growing to be the type of man who I am asking you to get over in an hour.

Stop Trying to Change These Men

Here is the deal, women are multipliers. We have the power to walk into a man's life and make him into more than he is presently. We also have the power to make him into everything that is already in him. Notice I said that is *already* in him. We were all born with unique and innate abilities. Some of us never get the chance to tap into them or to even explore them. This doesn't change the fact that it is in us. This means, you have the power to walk into a man's life and to influence and inspire him to reach his full potential. It is no wonder the bible says that he that findeth a wife findeth a good thing.

If you are that good thing, woman of God, why is it that the person you are trying to get over, doesn't realize this? And while you are pondering on that question, I want you to understand this: a man who truly loves you, will recognize his flaws, he will recognize that in order to keep this *good thing* that he has found, he has to become his highest self. If a man is not willing to become his highest self so that he can be the best man he can be to himself, you, and his family, then he does not deserve you. If he values you, he would see you as a treasure and would level up to keep you.

Here is where a lot of women go wrong though. Instead of walking away, we stay, and try to change the man. We try to force him to level up. We try to make him into something that he is telling you that he is not. This doesn't mean that we can't see the good in people, or the potential in people when they themselves don't see it. But when a man does not see his potential, and he has one of the character flaws that I listed earlier, you need not waste your time with him. Period.

Don't Fall Into the Trap

Please start believing men when they show you who they are through their actions. I don't care if he is telling you he loves you with his mouth. What are his actions saying? To the women who like fixer-uppers, please believe these men when they show you that they don't want to be fixed. And when they do show you this, please stop playing small to make them feel greater about themselves. Stop abandoning your dreams so that you don't intimidate the man who decided not to pursue his.

Please pull yourself from that net of mediocrity that you have fallen under. Be real with yourself. You know that you are greater than what you have settled for. You were called to a life with more substance. A bigger and more fulfilling life. Stop playing small to please someone who doesn't want to be great.

This is why you will notice a lot of times, when we leave a relationship, a lot of us begin to accelerate. When I walked away from my marriage, I gained things that the marriage had been blocking. I gained my business. My relationship with God was restored. I gained clarity on my life, and I found my purpose. My value had not decreased just because someone didn't see what I was worth. I was still the same Sileta who God had invested in. There was still a major mandate on my life.

This is why a lot of you are being prompted now to leave toxic relationships. You have a mandate on your life that requires more out of you. When you leave that relationship, you are giving yourself the opportunity to start fresh and to embark on a brand-new journey. Sometimes we go as far as cutting our hair so that we can get a new look, or we immediately go searching for a version of ourselves we abandoned a long time ago. The new you is calling!

The Women in Your Life

Because I had such a great relationship with my mom, it was hard for me to understand why so many of my female friends didn't have good relationships with their mothers. It baffled me to hear them talk about how their mothers envied them, hated them, deceived them, and the whole nine yards. Most of the time, a generational curse was the reason behind this pattern that kept passing down from one generation to the next.

What I find strange too, is that a lot of women have similar relationship patterns as do their moms. The mother wasn't married, and neither were they. The mother chased men away with her loud mouth, and the daughter now finds herself doing the same thing in her relationship. Or how about this one, the mother has been changing partners every six months, and now, that is the same cycle that the daughter has found herself in. Have you been noticing similarities in the patterns between you and your mother? What about between you and your daughter? Pay attention to these cycles. Never ignore them.

Who are you Having Babies With?

I find it strange that even when a child and their biological parent have been separated from one another for decades or forever, the child might still take on some of the mannerisms and behaviors of the parent, even without learning it from them. While some of these mannerisms, traits, and qualities may be good for some, others may be forced to take on the worst parts of their biological parents. This is why I am cautioned against having children for just any man. It is important to know the demons that this man is fighting with and what type of curses have been passed down from his father or mother, to him.

Just the same, you need to be very careful about who you get married to. Make sure he is saved and freed from any generational curses that might have attached themselves to him. When my ex husband's mother had learned about some of the things her son was doing to me, she shared with me that his father, even though he was not present in his life, had done some of the same things to her. The drinking, the anger, the violence. She also reminded me that it was she who had warned me not to marry him, the night we announced we were getting married. Would you believe me if I told you that I took it personal that she had told me not to marry her son? This woman was trying to save me! And I still didn't listen.

Is it possible that your husband, similar to his father, is struggling with infidelity, alcoholism, and perhaps even anger and violence? Of course we don't always get to know these things up front before dating someone. Not only that, but in some instances, if the person you are dating doesn't know anything about their father or mother's lineage, they might not understand themselves and some of the things they might be struggling with. This is why it is so important to know who you are letting into your life. It is even more critical to know exactly who you are having babies with.

Cancel the Generational Curses

Generational curses are cancelled through salvation. That's when we open our mouths, put down our feet, and say enough is enough. They are broken in our surrender to God. When we turn from our wicked ways. 2 Chronicles says, "If my people, which are called by my name, shall humble themselves, and pray, and seek my face, and turn from their wicked ways; then will I hear from heaven, and will forgive their sin, and will heal their land."

Even when these curses are broken, demons sometimes watch from a far for an opportunity to manifest once more in your life. This is why you have to remember to put on the whole armor of God. I want to warn you too, that when you defeat a demon, you do not want to re-open those doors again. Because when they return, they will do so seven times as strong. I don't know about you, but I'd rather beat it and get over it the first go around than to fight with it on round two. God's plan for you is that you prosper. He wants you to have life and to have it more abundantly. It is time you wake up, recognize the patterns in your life, and start bowing down before God in full surrender.

PART two

The Art of Letting Go

To the woman who can't forgive

Dear woman of God,

I can't tell you how many times I sat at my computer and tried to write this chapter, and just could not get the words out. I knew that God was having me to dedicate this chapter to the woman who was struggling with unforgiveness. I didn't have a clue that there were things that I was holding on to, that people had done to me, things that had happened in my life, that I hadn't forgiven. There were people who never said sorry, who I had to learn to pray for and forgive anyway.

Even when the other chapters were written, I couldn't figure out what God wanted me to do with this one. It wasn't until I went on a fast that he started speaking to me and he taught me about the dangers of not forgiving. Strange enough, he led me to a book my grandmother, Lottis Hodge, had written in the late 1980's, called *Ning's Troubles*. Her nick-name was Ning. I had read the book before, but this was the first time that I really understood the trauma that she had lived through.

My grandmother, at the age of 13, was struck down by Polio—a condition that held a reign of worldwide terror, especially at its peak in the 1950s, as it paralyzed and killed its victims. The condition left her disabled, with one hand locked in the wrist and numbness in one foot. She had to learn to talk and walk again. Today, she walks with a limp. Her story was deeper then polio, however. It was a story of a woman who learned to trust God no matter what turn her life was taking. The aftermath of it was a story of love and forgiveness. I talk about it in more details in the coming chapter. But I wrote this letter to tell you, you are not what happened to you.

When my grandmother came down with polio, she explained that it felt like her life had ended, that God was not with her. This one thing made every other area of her life ten times harder. The men in her life, including my grandfather, took advantage of her weakness and abused her. It was so easy for her to just curse God, if she wanted to. It was so easy for her to turn away from him. But instead, she found ways to give him thanks and praises.

You who are reading this, people may have taken advantage of you because of your condition. Maybe they took advantage of the fact that you were insecure, or young, or naïve. Sometimes people will make you a victim because they see that you have gone through some type of trauma already. Those are the people you are going to have to forgive.

It is not your fault that they did what they did to you, but how you respond to it is certainly your responsibility.

In this hour, God is telling you to forgive them and move on. It may not look like it, but God is still in control.

Stay blessed, my Sister.

CHAPTER

3

THE CUTTING AWAY *of Old Cloth*

WHEN I WAS A LITTLE GIRL, I enjoyed cutting old fabric in my mom's house, and out of that fabric, I would design dresses for my dolls. Next to reading, doing this placed me in a beautiful mental space, especially as I watched something that was lifeless become transformed by a piece of fabric. I would get approval from my mother on which fabrics I could cut, but it always made me nervous, because once I moved the blade through it, there was no turning back. She would hand me the cloth (usually the remains of an old sheet or curtain), the needle the thread, and then the scissors. Once they were all in my possession, I would begin cutting away, before she changed her mind. Now that I think of it, she only handed me the cloth that had been used, cloth that she didn't want. She never once gave me a piece of fabric that she valued. I want to ask you this question: Has someone handed you the scissors to cut through and sever a relationship that they no longer want? If they did, what are you waiting for? It is time to send the scissors through that mess of thing you call love, and to do so with a consuming eagerness to make something beautiful out of this new opportunity.

Get Angry. But Get Classy!

In William Congreve's 1697 poem, *The Mourning Bride*, he says, "Heaven has no rage like love to hatred turned, nor hell a fury like a woman scorned." Those lines carry so much weight and truth, and why do you think that is? Think about it, when we are hurt, we really have the capacity to pull the carpet from under a man's feet, to blow the roof from over his head, and to even light a match and set his life ablaze, even if that means we are going to catch a fire with him.

When a man hurts you, it is okay to feel pain, but it is time you stop letting these men see you burn. It is time you hold your heads up and go out there and do something you never did. The only revenge you are entitled to is becoming the best version of yourself. When a man walks away from you, the next time he runs into you or catches a glimpse of you, a part of him is supposed to say, *My God—look at what I missed out on*. Or, *why did I not realize that she had this in her all along*? Stop making a fool of yourself by calling him and begging him to come back, begging him to leave that woman alone, begging him to be there for you, even though he has shown and even told you that he does not love you. Stop letting your emotions get the best of you. No man is worth going to jail over. No man is worth losing your mind over. And no man is worth losing your self-respect over.

Some of you are waiting for an apology. He didn't apologize—*so what?* Accept the apology he never gave and raise your vibration above what he has done to you. Stop waiting for closure and start stitching up your own wounds. I could never forget the honesty of one of my friends in my early years of dating. I had come to the end of a relationship with someone I was very much in love with. I couldn't understand what had happened, but my friend who was dating his brother at that time, knew more than I did, and really, she didn't want to hurt my feelings. He had met someone else. This was the woman he wanted to be with. And he had to get rid of me. But he had made me so many promises. We went to church together on Sundays. I couldn't understand why it ended so abruptly. I was very young, and it was actually the first time I had ever been hurt by someone I loved. I kept talking about it, and when I wasn't talking, I was crying over him. I lost my appetite for months and had dropped so much weight, it looked unhealthy. My friend did a good job with cheering me up, but one day, she couldn't take it anymore. She finally let it out.

"*He doesn't want you*. Stop crying over him. *He is with someone else*. Get over him!" There was no easier way for her to bring it across to me.

My world stopped spinning in that moment. Her mouth was still moving, but my ears had stopped hearing. It was the first time someone had been so honest and raw with me. The words replayed in my ears—*he doesn't want you. He doesn't want you. He doesn't want you.* It was true. I got angry. Not with her. I needed that truth from her. That's what friends do. I wasn't even angry with him either. I was angry with myself for holding on to words that were said. I was angry that I had been so desperate to be loved. I was angry that I had spent so much time waiting for an explanation. I was angry that I had wasted so much time trying to fit in pieces to a puzzle that didn't need to be solved. We need to get to a point, women, where we realize that every problem might have a solution, but every problem doesn't need to be fixed. I made a decision in that moment to suck it up. To let it go. And to let God. I considered him my true first love. If I ever saw him again, I would say, *Thank you*.

It is time you started accepting the apology you never got. It is time you forgive him for what he has done to you. Again, if you are trying to start a new relationship, but haven't first accepted the fact that your last relationship has ended, then you need to take a step back, and let that person who is pursuing you know that you are not ready. Maybe you are the one doing the pursuing and the person is pulling back, and they are not telling you the reason why they are doing it. Their why, is not your business. You need to arrive at a place within where there is balance, wholeness, and peace. Get yourself in order. Whether you are a grown woman or a young woman, it is important that you learn responsibility. Start taking better care of yourself. Go into isolation. Take yourself out of the dating world, because the truth is, you are emotionally unavailable.

I used to hold on to the roses he bought me. Once they died, I would hold them in a vase and keep them in the window sill. It really amazes me how a rose holds its beauty, even when the sunlight can no longer give it life. I held on to those roses though, because they reminded me that I was not entirely crazy. The pain I was feeling didn't just conjure up itself. It came from somewhere. This person at one point, did convince me that he loved me. The roses were evidence of those words—*or so I thought*. The truth is, if he loved me, he would've chosen me. The more I was reminded of these things, the more I kept holding on to a time that had already passed. I had let go of him with my mouth, because I was no longer talking about him. But I needed to let him go in the other places where I had locked pieces and memories of him. One morning I grabbed the roses, took them down to a nearby lake, and one by one, I let them go.

You, my reader, also have things that you need to let go of that are keeping you soul-tied to a man who has handed you scissors and has told you that it is over. Even if he has never told you that, I am sure his actions have spoken it loudly. It is time to let go of him in all of the areas you have locked him up too. Some of you have things that you need to drag out of your house and pull down to the garbage dump and throw away. Release him from the firm grip you have held him in, and while you're at it, release him from your mind, your body, your spirit, and soul.

Do Something You've Never Done

When my divorce was finalized, I did something that I hadn't done the entire time I was with him. I got on a plane and I went to see my mother. Four years had passed since I had last seen her. My ex-husband didn't stop me from seeing her, but I will say this, being in that relationship stopped me from going anywhere. In life. Period. I couldn't explain why my finances were tied up, to the point that I went from being able to take care of myself and live on my own, to now having a second person in my household, and struggling some months to stop my cell phone from being turned off. Sometimes when you allow people to move under your roof, they move in with the demons and spirits that are attached to them as well.

Even though I had spoken with my mother nearly every day over that four-year period, seeing her in person was heart breaking. So much time had passed. So much had gone unsaid. There was so much that words alone couldn't capture. When we are caught up in the wrong relationship, we sometimes miss out on the people who really matter. That trip was the last trip I would make to the island of Nevis and see my mother alive. The following year, she passed away, just days before I was scheduled to fly in and see her again. It breaks my heart when I think of this sometimes. Where did all the time go? What a price to pay for being in the wrong relationship.

Some of you are literally missing out on opportunities to spend time with people in your life who can never be replaced. Perhaps you need to book a flight and go visit someone you haven't seen in years. Maybe it's your mother. Your father. Perhaps it's an old friend. Life is too short to not balance the hate with love, the pain with happiness, and the anger with peace. There is an art to letting a man Go. You need to learn it. And you need to learn it quickly. It starts with forgiving yourself, forgiving them, and finally, creating something beautiful from the pieces of you that are left.

Forgive Yourself

A lot of us struggle to forgive people from our past for the things they have done to us; still, a lot of times, we forget to forgive ourselves first. I struggled for the first two years of my mom's death, with the guilt of not taking the time to visit with her. Though I tried my best to financially support her, I didn't realize that my presence was far more important. I beat myself up for a while for not packing my things when I knew the relationship was over. I wondered if that would've made my mom happier. For sure it would have made me happier. Even though I didn't tell her what I was going through, she felt it, and had asked me to return home for a while.

"*You got to catch yourself*," she would say. It took me a while to realize that I was literally falling.

I felt guilty for not being there for her physically. I also felt guilty for not standing up for myself when I needed to. I had to learn however, that if we don't forgive the pain of our past, we will hold back our destiny. So I had to let go of that pain and guilt. And I had to forgive myself.

Some of you may not share the same guilt as I did, but maybe you feel guilty for abandoning your children, or for not pursuing your dreams. Perhaps the guilt you feel is for abusing your body and giving it away to men, just because they knew how to say *I love you*. Stop feeling guilty and start making it right. And if it is too late to make it right, forgive yourself and move on from it.

Girl—Forgive Him. Do it For You.

In his book, *The Forgiveness Project*, Michael S. Barry, approached the question of whether or not there was a relationship between cancer and the spirit of forgiveness. In the research that he and a team of other researchers carried out at the Cancer Treatment Centers of America, he stumbled upon the startling discovery that there indeed is a connection between our immune system and forgiveness. After examining a sample of cancer patients, it was determined that 61% of patients were struggling with unforgiveness. He explained that chronic anxiety was just one of the conditions that came about as a result of harboring these types of negative emotions.

Some of the men that we have let into our lives have done us some unimaginable harm, I agree. I have sat in the presence of plenty of women and listened to them talk about what they went through in a relationship. I have kept my mouth shut as a lot of them spoke. The truth is, nothing I've been through comes close to what some of them have endured. Some of them allowed men into their homes who raped and molested their daughters. Some of them were robbed by their own boyfriends, and other scammed by their husbands.

I recall some years back, meeting with an old college classmate who had just moved to Atlanta. She had just gotten married. Her husband was preparing to join her in Atlanta. He was moving from Jamaica. It didn't matter that I had just gone through a divorce. I was happy for her. It gave me hope. Months passed though, and I didn't hear her say much about him anymore. We would take long walks together through different nature trails, just to stay fit. She would talk about work, her aspirations, and how she was getting accustomed to Atlanta, but she didn't say much about him. I didn't ask either. We really weren't that close, but it was good to know someone in the same city.

She called me one day though and told me what was going on. It turned out that the man had only married her to get his green card. His entire family knew it, and they played along with it. The more she told me about her situation, the more strength she was building up within. Women are relational. She didn't tell me because she needed consoling. She was doing a great job with dealing with it internally. She had accepted it for what it was. Sometimes though, as women, we just need someone to talk to. Someone who won't judge us, won't laugh at us, won't beat us up. Someone who we can just have a glass of wine with and just sit down and rebuild. My first advice to her was "Girl, do not give him his papers!" She was about to file for both he and his daughter. But I learned something that day though. Sometimes it is okay to give someone exactly what they came for, and to keep it moving. She showed me that women are powerhouses. We are cut from a fabric that doesn't tear easily, and even when it is cut, we can stitch it back together and create something far more captivating.

A Visit With Ma

I paid a visit to my grandmother's house in Anguilla, one summer. I didn't tell her I was coming and had wearied myself in tapping on all the windows and doors, before realizing that she wasn't home. In the islands, we don't call before we show up at people's homes. We just pull up, honk the horn, knock on the doors and windows, then keep it moving, if no one responds.

When I didn't hear her answer, I hopped back into my rental, but before I could pull out onto the dirt road, I heard her calling to me. *But how the heck did she not hear me beating down the doors and where was her voice coming from?* It wouldn't be long before she emerged from the thick green bushes with her hair tied up in a wrap and a brown basket pressed against her hip.

"I was in me' ground, picking peas!" she raised her voice over the incessant bark of a black dog that had been violently hollering at me as it pressed against the neighbor's fence.

"Where ya' going?" she asked, before signaling me to roll back into the yard. The dog was still barking. I laughed as my grandmother called to it to hush and quiet down.

It was good to see her. I was always amazed by her energy and her ability to move around and keep herself busy. She didn't waste any time on catching up with my life either. She wanted to know what I had been eating that made me gain so much weight. She wanted to know what I was doing with my life in the States. Then finally, she got to the part where she wanted to know when I was going to find a man, get settled down, and have children.

"Well, you know I'm divorced now?" Those words were getting easier and easier for me to say.

She was very much taken back by my response. Not because she thought it was tragic that I had divorced. Even worse, she had no idea that I had gotten married in the first place. *Yes—I was that bad.* I apologized that no one had told her. Then again, I hadn't really told anyone. I didn't want to go too much into what happened, who the guy was that I had married, where he was from, and why it didn't work. The fact remained—it didn't work. She didn't press me either.

"You want Johnny Cake?" That was her way of saying stay a little longer. And if you, my reader, don't know what a Johnny Cake is, you haven't lived yet! That is yet another reason why you need to get over him in an hour.

I watched closely as she kneaded the dough and then pulled off chunks of the flour and flattened them before dropping them in the hot oil. When the first one was perfectly cooked and browned on both sides, she handed it to me on a saucer. I didn't waste any time breaking a piece off and throwing it into my mouth. It burned, but it was so *good and yummy—it was worth the burn!* My grandmother smiled as she watched me consume the Johnny Cake.

"You know how to make em, right?" she asked. I was embarrassed to say no. So I simply said, "Not the way you make em!" She knew I was lying.

"Well, you know how to cook, right?" she pried a little deeper, this time, with a little more concern in her voice. She didn't take her eyes off of the cakes. Another two were ready to leave the pan and I watched as she stuck a two-pronged fork into them and transferred them to a plate to cool.

"Of course," I said. I was honest this time. I knew how to cook. Just not Johnny Cakes.

"Oh—you betta!" she warned, "You gon' have to cook for your husband and children someday." I laughed at her comment. But she didn't stop there.

"Don't you want a family one day?" It wasn't a conversation I wanted to have with her at all. I really just wanted to eat my Johnny Cake. I stuffed the other half of it in my mouth and pointed to it to show her I was eating. She left the subject alone and went on to talking about someone she was taking care of on her job. I was always amazed by how much my grandmother was able to accomplish on her own, especially after all she had been through.

She had lost two homes to a fire, at two different times in her life. In those days, people without electricity in their homes were vulnerable to fires. Not all homes were made of concrete either. Some were wooden. A kerosene lamp lit up rooms, most nights. Sometimes a candle did the job. She didn't just lose homes though. On multiple occasions, she lost bits and pieces of herself. Literally.

When she was seventeen, she was raped by a man and got pregnant as a result. From this rape, she bore her second child. Her first child came at the age of 14, a year after she was struck by polio. The man who raped her was my grandfather. Afraid to tell anyone what had happened to her, an abusive relationship ensued between the two. It was a relationship that gave her life, as she bore a total of four children for him. But that same relationship on many occasions, nearly took her life.

83

Despite her disability, this man had brutally beaten her—even while she was pregnant, strangled her until her tongue was sticking out of her mouth, held her head under water in attempts to drown her. It didn't stop there either. Each time he attacked her, sometimes beating her until urine streamed down her legs, she told herself she wouldn't let him back into her life, but her Grandmother would encourage her to go back. At one point, her grandmother even told her that her sister Victoria had survived fourteen stabs from her husband and she still stayed and made the relationship work. This meant that my grandmother wasn't experiencing anything worth complaining about.

She shouldn't have let him in on the night of August 3rd, however. She was at her grandmother's house that night, alone with her children, when he showed up. I imagine he apologized and said something sweet, and she let him in. In her book, she explained that he made love to her that night. Then immediately after, he took a pair of scissors and stabbed her four times. Her belly was hanging out four inches as she trailed a long dirt path that night, holding on to dear life, hoping to make it to the nearest house to ask for help.

Before I released this book, I got a chance to speak with my dad and to hear his version of this story. It is amazing how when something tragic happens to us, there are other voices who have stories that have stemmed from these tragedies too. Very often, it is our children who have those stories. He was asleep when what could've been his mother's murder, was taking place. He woke up soaked in blood. The other children were crying and in shock. All he could remember them saying was, "She's dead! *Ma* is dead!"

"It was a complete horror!" he exclaimed.

But there she was, standing in the kitchen, hopping around on one foot, making Johnny Cakes with one hand. The roof over her head was a testament of God's love and grace. She had managed to build that home with her youngest daughter, while working overseas as a caretaker to an elderly man in New York City.

"She's a superwoman," my dad explained. "Strength like that can only come from a superwoman."

You have to understand that it takes just as much strength to stay in an abusive situation as it does to leave it. I wanted to talk to my grandmother before completing this chapter. I really wanted to ask her one thing: *Did you forgive him*? Her answer was priceless.

"Forgiving him was the only way that I was able to emancipate myself and truly experience the love of God."

That night, while my grandmother slept, I sat on the porch and looked out at the sky. The heat from earlier in the day was still rising from the concrete, and it was giving my bare feet a soothing massage as I moved them back and forth. My ears still weren't used to the sound of the chirping crickets and all the other creatures whose voices had been tugging at them. The faithful moon was pressed against the night and the stars had come out to paint freckles across the sky. This was home sweet home.

I thought of my own life, and the relationships I had in the past. I realized that just as the right people can bring blessings into our lives, the wrong ones can bring curses. My prayer became this: *Lord, please bless me with the man* you *have for me. I don't want nothing more or less. Everything else, please cut it away. Even if it hurts. Cut it away.*

To the abused woman

Dear Woman of God,

One of the coolest things I think I ever did in my early twenties, was help a friend of mine move out of her apartment. I say it was cool, but now that I think of it, it was thrilling, and maybe even dangerous. But in the moment, it was cool. We had less than an hour to move her out of an apartment she shared with her boyfriend. I don't recall him being physically abusive towards her, but he was verbally and mentally abusive, and she had had enough of it. She was afraid to leave him though. But she knew she had to leave. She planned it carefully. Waited for him to leave for work, kissed him goodbye, meanwhile myself and maybe 4 others were on our way, one with a truck to stack the large items, the others with our cars.

When she gave us the call that we were clear to come, we pulled up, went upstairs, each person grabbing whatever she handed to us. In an hour, we were in and out of there. Before we left, I stood in the door-way with her and looked into the apartment where so many dinners, game nights, and fun moments had been shared. The space was

87

leased in his name, but when they moved in, she was the one with the furniture.

All of her belongings were now crammed into the second room of my apartment. I remember sitting next to her later that evening, trying to console her, when her phone started ringing. It was him. She answered it with a smile. He was wailing on the other end. He had come home to an empty apartment. He never thought she would have the strength to leave. He begged her to come back. She never did. Lucky for her, she was working and able to take care of herself. Some of you reading this, won't have time to pull off something like what she had done. Some of you will have to go just as you are.

I get it though. The reason why a lot of you haven't left that relationship is because you are fearing that you won't have the provision to take care of yourself. Maybe you have children with this person and so walking away just doesn't seem like the answer. So instead, you have remained in a state of false imprisonment, you have made a bed on shattered glass, without realizing that you are in danger. Of all the chapters I have written in this book, this by far is the most urgent, because your failure to move forward in this moment could cost you your very life. Your unique suffering is that the enemy has crippled your mind and told you that there is nowhere for you to run. Don't you know that God provides for even the birds of the air? You, my sister, are far more valuable to him than they are. Don't you know he will do much more for you? Take a second to read Matthew 6:26. Memorize and take it with you on this journey. God loves you, my sister, and he will make a way for you. He is always several steps ahead of us, but you won't be able to meet him, if you don't begin taking the first steps forward.

He is calling you out of that relationship where a man has been constantly abusing you physically, emotionally, and even spiritually. He sees your open wounds and is calling you to a place of complete healing. He has heard your cries in the midnight hours. He has seen your tears as they fell to the ground; some soaked in your pillow. This is not his will for you. But he will turn it around for his glory.

Can I get an amen?

CHAPTER

4

"STEP OVER THE Shattered Glass"

I **WATCHED MY HUSBAND**, who was abusive and cold towards me, break down in tears after receiving a phone call from a friend of his. Immediately I knew that something devastating had happened. I silenced the music that was playing in the background, washed my hands from seasoning meat, then walked over to him to find out what was wrong. He stood in front of me, looking off to the side, and almost frozen. Finally, when he was able to speak, I felt every hair on my body rise up. Nothing could have prepared me for what I had just heard. A close female friend of his was tragically killed. She was shot in the head by her husband. Her mother, who was in the house at the time, was shot and killed too. Their six-year-old daughter managed to run through the front door, across to the neighbor's home, where she was desperately pounding her fists against the door, begging to be let in. Before they could let her in, another shot went off. By the time the cops arrived, three dead bodies had been laid out in cold blood.

As we entered the venue where the wake was being held, I crossed my arms and rubbed both of my shoulders, in an attempt to shake off the eerie feeling that was engulfing me. We followed a loud wailing voice through the halls, until we found the room where the wake was being held. Two beautiful white caskets with gold trimmings were positioned at the front of the room. Both of them were closed. The woman whose voice we heard, was sitting in a chair, her head leaned into the stomach of another woman who was standing over her and trying to soothe her.

A few people greeted us with sad and helpless eyes. I tried to understand what had happened. What type of war of the mind would make a man come home and turn the gun on his wife, her mother, and then himself? How troubled does one have to be that they would go as far as taking someone's life if that person tried to leave them?

A week before the young woman and her mother were murdered, my ex-husband and I had visited their home where we were served warm and freshly made oatmeal cookies. Their daughter, a bright-eyed little girl named Annie, who pronounced my name *S-A-LEE-TAH* was bouncing around the house with a doll in her hand. I even had a chance to meet the husband, who sat with us for a while and kept a worth-while conversation going. At one point, his wife pulled out an old album with photos of her brother, who they had lost tragically, a few years earlier. I could see the pain of losing a son in the mother's eyes, even though she smiled and laughed as everyone exchanged their best memories of him. The brother was a very close friend of my ex-husband as well.

From what I observed, they seemed like a happy family. There were no cries for help in anyone's eyes that day. The house was filled with the sweet smells of cookies, creased eye-corners from constant smiling, and laughter that echoed through the halls from the little girl who was busy entertaining her doll. I wondered whether or not the husband had been abusive to his wife in the past. And if he was, did she ever for a second think that it was going to go this far? The truth is, when we stand face to face with someone we love who is spitting these unflinching threats at us, we seldom believe that they will actually go that far. Cognitive dissonance sets in. We try to reason with ourselves and find evidence that says he won't.

In my own marriage, I listened to my ex-husband as he held a gun to his own head and threaten to kill himself if I wouldn't agree to stay with him. This all started when he arrived home one night and found that I wasn't there. Not only that, but that I had left with most of my clothing. I was sitting in a friend's parking lot and getting ready to pull my bags out, when my phone rang. He was crying. He was saying that he would kill himself. I was afraid that he would. I went back. I walked into the apartment and found him in one corner, sitting against the wall. The gun was next to him. I kept asking myself, *when had things gotten this grave between us? When had this become my story*?

I stayed, and for a while, things had calmed down. But the devil prowls even in the stillness. I stuck around long enough to see that same gun being pointed to my own face—at which point, the only thing standing between my life and my death, was God's mercy.

I overheard a few people at that wake talking about the double-homicide. One woman in a whispered voice was explaining to two or three other women that her friend was planning to leave her husband, and when he found out, he told her that he couldn't live without her. A lot of times when we are planning to leave a toxic relationship, we try to pick up the broken pieces on our way out. Sometimes we need to leave those pieces right there and make do with what is left of us.

If you my reader, have found yourself in this position, I am warning you now, do not entertain threats when you are in a relationship. If someone says they will kill you, believe them. If they say they cannot do without you—get out! It is not cute. It is not to be taken lightly. Leave that relationship. Get yourself and your family to shelter. If you have no family, find a shelter in your local city or move farther away. It is better to leave with nothing but your life, than to stay and allow someone who has nothing else to live for, take your life, and the lives of others around you.

Speak to Someone About it

The more violent the offense, which 31% of cases are, the more likely the woman will not report it; that is according to a report presented to the public by The Bureau of Justice Statistics. This is because women fear reprisal. We don't want the attacker to return. A lot of times we are protective of the attacker too. I can't tell how many times I have called the police on my ex-husband. When they arrived, he was in tears. He told the officers how much he loved me and that it was only a simple altercation. Most of the times, the officers asked me to give him a chance. Y*es, they did*. Only once did an officer pull me aside and tell me don't be stupid. Press charges. But I was stupid. I was more worried about what that would do to his job, what his mother would think of me, what other people would say; I was hardly worried about myself. I was foolish, but this is the mental war that a lot of women in domestic situations go through.

When we are forced to let go of something we love, are attached to, or are even obsessed with, this can easily usher in a state of emotional distress. I made sure that I did not prescribe a one-size fit all list or steps for getting over a relationship to you because I understand that we all deal with things differently. We are affected by life-changing events in a number of ways. Some of us are able to wipe our tears today and start over tomorrow. The rest of us may need more time. This becomes all the more complicated when other people like children and in-laws are involved.

I don't think it takes an hour to get over someone you have loved for years. But really, you need less than an hour to make your mind up that you are going to move on. Most of us take too much time to say enough, to walk away, and to get through the grieving process. We often spend too much time crying over something that has expired. For some of you, the man has already moved on. Already married someone else. Already started a family. Two years have passed. Ten years have passed. What exactly are you holding on to?

Again, our coping mechanisms are all different. We stem from different cultures. We have different experiences that impact how we respond to certain stimuli. Some of you are holding on because you are afraid of how others will look at you once you are divorced or you are afraid that you will be condemned or frown upon for walking away, even when the man is chronically unfaithful, deathly abusive, and outright disrespectful. Some of you may not have a strong support system or someone you can speak and reason with about what it is that you are going through. A lot of times women, we turn to friends and family for advice, only to have those same friends use what we have shared with them, against us.

I don't ever talk about this, but I recall when I was going through my divorce, my closest friend at that time and I got into an argument, and in that moment, she threw everything I had shared with her about my husband and his infidelity, in my face. I forgave her, but I learned a major lesson that day— KEEP YOUR BUSINESS TO YOURSELF.

The truth is though, we all need someone to talk to and to reason with. Sometimes, your support system is better off being a stranger. And by that, I mean, a licensed counselor or therapist. Some of you may keep a journal as a form of therapy and some of you might prefer to just take it to the Lord in prayer. Along with those two, I am also advising you to seek out a human therapist who can help you to sort through some of the things you are struggling with. Going through a break-up, a separation, or a divorce, is not easy. It is especially difficult when you have children involved. The only thing worse than going through this severing, is not having the mental strength to leave in the first place, even when the situation has become life-threatening. If you find yourself in this position, go get help. Carry out an online search and look for non-profits in your area that offer free assistance for these problems. Some of you reading right now will be the people that God raise up to open these types of non-profits in your local communities. Don't sit there feeling sorry for yourself, girl. Trust me, you got a lot to live for.

Battered Woman Syndrome

When a woman has endured serious, long-term domestic abuse, this can lead to a mental disorder known as battered woman syndrome, which is a sub-category of post-traumatic stress disorder

(PTSD). A woman suffering from battered woman syndrome is often characterized as having some form of learned helplessness where she begins to think that she deserves the abuse she is receiving and that there is no way to get away from it. It is hard for women to regain control once they get to this mental point. This is usually one of the reasons why the abuse goes unreported.

The women who develop battered woman syndrome typically journey through four stages, and I want to point these stages out so that it might help you to recognize whether or not this is your situation.

1. *Denial:* in this stage, the woman has a difficult time accepting the fact that she is in an abusive relationship. One of the ways she justifies the abuse is by explaining that he has never done that before and he only did it that *one time.*

2. *Guilt*: as the woman advances from denial to guilt, she starts to believe that she is the cause of the abuse that has been inflicted upon her. Some women may find themselves saying things like, *if I wasn't like this, he wouldn't be like that, or if I learn to do this, he would stop doing that.*

3. *Enlightenment:* After the guilt phase, comes a period of enlightenment. This is the stage where the woman begins to realize that she really does not deserve to be treated in the way she has been. She begins to realize that her partner is indeed "abusive". She also begins to realize that she has been manipulated into seeing and thinking otherwise. Her eyes are also opened, at this point, to the level of control that she has been under.

4. *Responsibility:* This is the stage where a lot of women struggle to get to. It is the stage where the woman realizes that her partner is the one who is responsible for what he has done and that it is not her fault. She also realizes that she needs to leave the relationship. Sadly, because domestic violence can become fatal, a lot of women never even make it past the third stage, much less the fourth.

As a survivor of an abusive relationship, I walked away with issues that I had to figure out how to cope with. Anxiety and depression were two of them. The National Institute of Mental Health has confirmed that one in five adults in the United States live with a mental illness. Less than half of those individuals have sought out or received treatment for their condition. One of the reasons for this is that there is a social stigma associated with mental illness. Once again, we are often so pre-occupied with how others view us, that it cripples us and prevents us from getting the help we need. Another reason many women don't seek out help for things like anxiety and depression is because they don't have access to care. Money is often a major barrier as well.

Very often too, we don't realize just how severe the situation that we are caught up in, is. The National Coalition Against Domestic Violence has warned that homicide risk in domestic violence is increased by 500% when there is a gun present, 72% of all murder-suicides involve an intimate partner, and 94% of victims are females. In a separate study on intimate partner homicides, it was determined that 20% of victims were not even the partners themselves, but they were people who jumped in to help. This includes family members, friends, and even law enforcement officers.

Next to battered woman syndrome, there are a plethora of physical, mental, and even sexual, and reproductive effects that are tied to domestic violence. Due to forced intercourse, some women are vulnerable to contracting STDs, including HIV, whereas, if it wasn't forced, they might have protected themselves or not had intercourse to begin. There is also a close relationship between intimate partner violence and depression, even suicidal thoughts. Minority Nurse Magazine has also shared that though intimate partner violence affects women from all races, socioeconomic backgrounds, and all ethnicities, minority women face the highest risk, at a rate of 35% higher than that of white women. Not only that, but these women are less likely to seek out assistance from women's programs. If you or someone you know is struggling with intimate partner violence, it is important that you speak up and get help.

It is Not Your Fault

Sometimes, being in an abusive relationship can put you in a place of mental isolation. This is not just for physical abuse. Mental abuse puts you in that space too. I want you to know that if you identify with this chapter in anyway, that it is not your fault that you have been abused by your partner. I want you to know that you are not alone. In the United States, every minute that passes, 20 people experience intimate partner violence, that is according to the National Coalition Against Domestic Violence. That's over 10 million victims each year. The same source has also confirmed that 20,000 calls are received by domestic violence hotlines on a typical day. I point these statistics out to show you that this is a real problem. And to also show you that help is out there. You are not alone.

I want to point out too, that the most dangerous time for a woman who is facing intimate partner violence, is the moment she expresses her desire to separate from him. Be wise, girl. Sometimes you need to step over the shattered glass and just go. When I say the shattered glass, I mean, you need to go at the first warning signs that your partner is abusive. I realize that a lot of us don't find this out until we have moved in under the same roof with this person, or until we have married this person. That is why it is so important to take time to get to know people. In either case, the moment you find this out, it doesn't matter where you are—you need to go. You are stronger than you realize. Tap into your superwoman strength and go.

Sadly, in my own experience, I never felt as though law enforcement could do enough to protect me. The idea of a restraining order didn't make me feel safe enough either. At one point, I decided that I wasn't going to leave; instead, I would fight back. What that almost did was put me in a position where I was almost arrested—and suddenly the tables turned. When I was done with him, he was the one who looked like the victim. Take my word for it: the best thing for you to do is walk away from these situations. Call law enforcement. Press charges. Get the restraining order. But most importantly—Get out!

Get Out of Your Comfort Zone

Comfort is perhaps one of the worst poisons we can swallow, because when we grow comfortable with a situation, we are resistant to change—even when it is necessary for our own survival. No one said you will stop loving the person. It is also very likely that you will miss this person. Here's the thing though, you have to start becoming uncomfortable with them hurting you. You have to put your foot down. You have to arrive at the point where you're uncomfortable with being comfortable with the abusive behavior. A lot of times because we find ourselves struggling to heal the pain we ask God to change our partner and make him a better person. When we don't hear God's voice, we wonder if God even exists. Well here's your answer, he does exist. He just can't live in the mess he's been calling you out of. While you're praying to him to help that relationship to work out, God is asking you to leave the pain and the partner, and go. Do you really think that that abusive man is what God wants for you.

The only survivors of a domestic violence relationship are those who are able to walk away from it—without turning back. I don't care if he has changed. I don't care if he completed a court-ordered anger management course. I don't care if he bought you 5 dozen roses and apologized to you in front of the whole world. It is just too much of a risk to go back. This is especially for those of you who were physically abused to the point you had to plan your get away. Remember, if you go back, he has already studied you. You got away the first time. You may not get away the next time. And I want you to understand this too; I believe people should be forgiven for hurting us and I believe people can change. Still, there are people who you need to walk away from and leave right where they are, without turning back. The moment they lay hands on you is the moment that their part in your story should be over. I know that is hard for a lot of you to accept, but you need to understand that you are worth far more than a man putting his hands on you. I think Judge Lynn Toler said it best in her book *Making Marriage Work*, "One blow. You Go. That's it. You do so intelligently, having gotten in touch with organizations that understand the complexities and dangers of leaving. But you go."

We have to find our healing. And we have to let these men find their healing too. Holding on to them, telling them you miss them, going back to them after they've said they're sorry—none of that is cute. You need to learn self-control, self-respect, and you need to develop a sense of self-worth. If that man is to ever change, it is very unlikely that it will happen while he is with the person who he has victimized. The very sight of you is supposed to be a reminder of how bad of a person he has been. It is counterproductive to the healing process for both of you. Move on!

Is it a Wound or a Scar?

A lot of us are carrying around open wounds. Some of us are carrying around scars. But we don't always realize the difference. An open wound is an injury that has not yet been healed. How many times have you taken back a man into your life who has an open wound? When I say open wound, I'm talking about a man who is still struggling with a drinking problem, for instance, or a man who still hasn't learned how to keep his hands off of you. Of course you never really know that someone has learned from their mistake until they are put to the test. Do you really want to find out if he will put his hands on you again though?

Scars represent the healing of a wound that was once open. They are a sign that at some point there was trauma. Women who have survived abusive relationships need to walk away with their wounds and allow those wounds to scar and to let those scars be a reminder of something they survived. It may be an ugly scar, but at some point you will

106

have the opportunity to make it into something beautiful. As for that man who has hurt you, if he ever changes, let your absence be a reminder to him that he should never be so foolish, unbalanced, or disturbed, so as to make that same mistake in relationships going forward. As for you and him, that chapter is closed. Move on with your wounds. Embrace your scars.

God Will Always Provide

I often find myself between two fires when discussing intimate partner violence. On one end, I am showing tough love to the woman, and trying to encourage her to walk away from the relationship. On the other end, I find myself defending the woman, only because I have been there. I understand what goes through the mind when your gut is telling you to go, but your deceitful heart is telling you to stay. We stay for a lot of different reasons. One of the reasons a lot of women stay is because of their socioeconomic status and perhaps more defeating, their mental status. Once a man is able to manipulate his victim and gain control over her mind, he is able to grip her into a strong hold. But how do a lot of us find ourselves at this place?

Recently, a group of researchers carried out a cross-sectional study on over 500 women in Iran. The aim of the study was to draw a comparison of the socioeconomic status, the perceived social support, and the mental status in women of reproductive age who were both experiencing and not experiencing domestic violence. What the study found was that 43% of the women surveyed, confirmed that they did experience at least one case of domestic violence. The study also found that domestic violence was more prevalent when the participants were younger, less educated, and when they stemmed from homes that were socioeconomically challenged.

Even when I was able to provide for myself financially, I did not have the mental strength to go. And so I can imagine that a woman without a financial means may find it twice or three times as hard to leave. And that's why I encourage you to seek out local resources where you can get help. Also, tell someone what you are going through. Don't fight this battle alone. Don't let the fear that there will be no provision trick you into staying either.

I moved to Atlanta twice. When I moved the first time, I stayed two years, but then my mother passed suddenly, and I ended up traveling to the island of Nevis for her funeral. The impact of what happened hit me so hard, I stayed overseas for nearly two years just trying to put the pieces back together. But one day, God said to me, it is time to

stop mourning and go where I have sent you.
Reminds me of the scripture 1 Samuel 16:1 where
God asked Samuel, *How long will you mourn Saul*?
A lot of times we prefer to sit in what happened to
us and we have a hard time separating ourselves
from the trauma. So much that we make it the
epicenter of our lives. We let it ferment and drag us
down. That's a part of the enemy's plan. He wants
you to live and then die in the mess around you.
That relationship that has been consuming your
time, your thoughts, it has been stopping you from
going forward, that spirit that has kept you stagnant,
it is time to abandon it. That's right. Abandon it and
go get your life back.

Following God's orders to return to Atlanta,
called for a lot of faith. In the time that I was away,
a lot of things happened. I lost my car. I no longer
had a home to return to. He was asking me to start
from scratch—literally, and he gave me a deadline
to do it by. I booked my flight, without having a
clue as to where I was going. I kept asking God,
*where am I going to stay? Am I going to be able to
afford it? Business is not the same! I don't have
first, last, and security to move into a new place.
Which property manager is going to approve me
with my bad credit?*

Maybe two weeks before my move, while I was
asleep, there was a loud thump on the door. It woke

me up. It was around 3am. I was a bit nervous because I was renting an apartment by myself on a very isolated part of the island of Anguilla. It was so quiet there, when the sea breeze blew you could hear loose items sweeping back and forth in the yard. I don't have a fearful spirit, but the knock sent me to the door, bent over and with wobbling knees. When I peeped out, there was no one there. No car. Nobody. Nothing. Only the shadow of palm trees swaying in the wind. That's when God said to me, *I need you to go online and find your apartment.*

I obeyed God's voice, pulled out my laptop and started searching for apartments. I happened to come across the name and number of a leasing agent. God said, *write it down and call her in a few hours.* As soon as 9 a.m. hit, I called her. I will never forget how our conversation went.

She said to me, "I don't care what your situation is, send in your application, and if you can get here by the 10th, I am moving you in with no money down and your first month FREE." Would you believe me if I told you that my flight was booked in advance, and I was scheduled to arrive in Atlanta on the 9th? This was the day God had told me to book it for. Some of you, God is calling you to a Genesis 22 type of faith, where Abraham took his only son Isaac to the land of Moriah and followed God's orders which said to sacrifice him as a burnt offering. When his son asked him if there is no sheep, Abraham told him that God will provide one. Abraham then built an altar and arranged wood on it, then tied his son and laid him on the altar. In the 10th verse, it explains that he lifted his knife to kill his son, and that's when the angel of the Lord called to Abraham from heaven and told Abraham not to lay hand on the boy. God was only testing his faith.

Sounds savage right? But how many of you are willing to look stupid for God? You've done it for a man. Some of us have done it for plenty of men. But are you willing to do it for God? I booked a flight to Atlanta for a date God asked me to book for. I had no idea where I was going to go after I stepped outside of that airport. But I had heard his voice clearly, and he told me to go to Atlanta. If you are wondering whether or not God will provide for you where you are going, I am telling you he will. But it requires a lot of obedience on your end. Go where God is leading you, and he will take it from there. You may arrive wounded. You may arrive with splinters in your feet. The only thing that matters is that you go.

To the woman in the wrong

Dear woman of God,

After reading through the coming chapter, I realized that the real problem that some women have is not the man, but more so, the problem is that they do not have self-control. This problem is also known as addiction. When you are addicted to a certain type of behavior or feeling, it is hard to break it. That is why you kick and throw a tantrum when something comes to an end. This is why you run into a new relationship before you can completely heal from a previous one. It is almost as though you are addicted to pain. Of all the chapters in this book, the one you are about to read is the only chapter where the woman is forced to accept responsibility for her wrongdoings, her bad ways, and for her role in ruining a relationship.

The reason you are suffering so much and are having a hard time letting go is because you realize that it was your fault that the relationship ended, and while you want a chance to prove yourself again, the man has moved on. You have to find peace with the situation, forgive yourself, and move on too. This new season of your life is a season where you will have to start looking at yourself. Start identifying your strong and weak areas. Some of you will need to start asking yourself, what is it that I really want? And, am I even ready for what it is I have been asking for?

You will be forced to look back at your previous relationships and look for patterns of bad behaviors and maybe even bad choices. You will have to forgive yourself. You will need to work on your character. You will also begin to learn that the reason that God is putting you through this season of self-discovery, is because He doesn't want you to miss out on the blessings that He is ready to release to you. What God has for us is for us, but we have to understand that some never get these things, because we run out of time. How long will you stay in your wilderness? As I am writing this letter, I can see a highway in the spirit and you traveling on it. I also see an exit in sight. That exit, my sister, is your exit to step into the blessings that God has in store for you. Will you be getting off on the next exit, or will you have to catch it the next time around? Here's a prayer that I wrote for you. Please read it out loud:

Dear Lord, please forgive and free me of any sin that I am not aware of. Free me of any soul ties, strong holds, spiritual husbands, un-Godly relationships. I bind the spirit of depression, of despair, and of stagnancy that has been attached to my life, and that has kept me repeating the same cycles, over and over.

I declare and decree that in this hour, I am free. I will go where you are leading me, Lord. I will do exploits. Everything that I have been through will be used for your glory. I will praise you through the pain and the hurt. Even the pain and hurt that I have inflicted upon myself through the bad choices I have made. I will trust in you Lord, even when things don't seem to be working out for my good.

I declare that the atmosphere in my home is shifting, the atmosphere in my mind is shifting, and the atmosphere in my spirit is shifting, even now. I declare that this is the day that the Lord has made. This is the hour that my life is turning around. The plan that the enemy has devised for my life is cancelled right now, in the name of Jesus.

Lord, I release any addictions, any ungodly relationships, and any demonic attachments in my life. I declare that I am free, in this hour.

In Jesus name, Amen.

God bless you, my sister.

CHAPTER

5

IT IS NOT THEM. It is you.

NEVER SEEK OUT A NEW relationship without first working on the parts of you that have been broken. Your aim should be to arrive to an inward destination of wholeness. It is not cute, admirable, or advisable to step into a relationship, hauling a load of emotional baggage to dump off on someone else. It is not fair to expect the new person to fix everything that went wrong in your life either. The ending of a relationship marks the beginning of something new, but it is not the ideal time to start dating or to get intimate with someone. Instead, this is the time when you should start falling back in love with yourself. It should be a time for you to start interviewing yourself. A time of discovery and getting to know you so that when you do meet that man that you've been praying for, you will also be that woman that he has been praying for. If you don't take the time to do this, you may very well be setting yourself up for continuous disappointment.

If your thoughts are still consumed by this person, if you talk about them every opportunity you get, and if you still haven't forgiven them, you are not ready to move on with someone new. I recall a time when I was getting to know a man whom I was mildly interested in. I say mildly because at that point in my life, I was all about my business and getting Sileta in order. The man was a business owner, very affluent, and he opened my eyes to the art of being business savvy. He was pursuing me to be his girlfriend, and while I was only mildly interested, I noticed very early in the friendship that he needed a friend more than he needed a girlfriend. We would meet for breakfast, lunch, sometimes dinner, and while we had very enriching conversations, every opportunity he got, he was talking about a woman who had broken his heart when he found out that she was cheating with an athlete. I couldn't tell which was hit more—his ego—or his heart. But I found the stories he shared to be quite interesting. I offered him advice on how he could move on from it. But I was also honest with him. I let him know that he should not be looking for a new relationship at this time. He needed to get over this woman first. In the meantime, he needed to focus more on himself, spend time with his children, and work on new ways to build his business. From this conversation, a beautiful friendship bloomed. And he did take my advice. Years later, he met a beautiful woman who he is now married to and have started a family with. Can you imagine how things would have went otherwise, if I had allowed him to forge a relationship with me?

If we don't recognize the seasons we are in, if we fail to place people into the right categories in our lives, we will always find ourselves mismatched and we will miss out on opportunities for deep and meaningful friendships. There is no reason why we should be so desperate for love that just about anybody will do. This is our lives we are talking about here. We only get one of those. We have to take better care of ourselves. We have to put ourselves in a better position so that when a real opportunity to love shows up, we will be ready, and that opportunity will find us.

The Need to Be Loved

You may be reading this and saying, *yeah well Sileta, I hear you, but I'm Lonely, and I need someone to keep me balanced.* When you isolate the man from the equation, you will realize that what you are really saying is that you have a need for love and a need for belonging that has not yet been met. The need to be loved is an intrinsic human desire. In 1943, American psychologist, Abraham Maslow, proposed a paper called, "A Theory of Human Motivation", which in short, was a theory of psychological health that was predicated on ideas of how humans prioritize their needs.

What Maslow proposed in this theory was that motivation is the attempt of humans to fulfill our five basic needs. These needs include our physiological needs—so food, water, shelter. Our needs for safety, our needs to socialize and to connect with others. Then there are our esteem needs, which include the need to feel respected and to gain the admiration of others. The last need he identified in this theory was the need to self-actualize. This is where as humans, we aim to reach our full potential. It was Maslow's belief that these needs manifest in a hierarchical order, where once the lower level needs are met first, there is a desire for the higher-level needs to be met. This theory has been praised in the business world, especially as managers try to understand the behavior of their employees. Because the theory is universal, it can be applied outside of the business world, and examined against other constructs, like relationships.

If you look at the pyramid that Maslow has framed his theory in and consider the position of the need for loving and belonging, and then self-esteem, which is the level above, we stumble upon a very telling paradox. It suggests that human beings conjure up the desire to be loved before they have the need or desire to feel some sense of self-worth, value, or accomplishment. I think that this pre-occupation with needing to be loved by someone else, forces us to forget that we must love ourselves first.

A lot of times as women, we are looking to men to tell us we are beautiful, when we ourselves don't even believe that we are. One of the reasons we can't believe that we are is because we feel that men often go after the most beautiful woman in the room; And, because we have often been the one who was not selected, we associate that with being the least attractive or less desirable.

Researcher and biological anthropologist, Helen Fisher, Ph.D., in one study, surveyed over 5,000 men and women to examine their dating preferences. The research confirmed that men have a desire for strong, smart, and successful women. Roughly 86 percent of the men surveyed reported that they were seeking a woman who was both confident and self-assured. This isn't to say that all men can handle a woman with all of these qualities—smart, successful, and driven. Also, not all women work, and so for some women, your admirable attributes may be identified in how well you keep a home, how well you raise your children, and how well you prepare a great meal.

If where you currently are in your life doesn't bring you a sense of accomplishment and security, I am encouraging you to find new things to do that will bring you that sense of accomplishment. I want to advise you too, that this doesn't come from a man. Our partners should bring us a sense of fulfillment in several areas of our lives, yes. They should make us feel loved, they should make us feel a sense of security. They should keep us warm in the cold winters. They should take out the trash. They should contribute to or pay the bills. They should add substance to our core being and impact our overall life experience.

Before that partner comes along, however, it is important that you have already brought yourself some level of fulfillment. It is important that you already have a sense of wholeness. Sure, it doesn't always happen in that order, but a lot of you are seeking a partner and you've been asking God where is he? Where is my Boaz? God is saying, He's coming. But I need you to get ready first. But how can you truly fix yourself if you don't even realize that there is a problem?

How Well do you Know Yourself?

You may be thinking, *well, if he hasn't showed up by now, that must mean, he is not coming*. This type of thinking can keep our heads under water, so much that we often don't realize that we are the ones blocking our own blessings.

I want to give you a little activity. Some of you may need a pen and paper for this. Some of you may need a day or two of pondering before you can come up with the answers. I want to ask you a series of questions, and I want you to answer each of them in complete honesty. It's not like I can see your answers. So be real with yourself.

1) Am I in good spiritual shape?
2) Am I expecting a man to save me?
3) Am I emotionally healthy at this point in my life?

Let's talk about how you answered the first three questions. The first question is focused on your spiritual well-being. I sincerely believe that the first relationship you have to get right, is your relationship with God. The bible says that we must seek ye first the kingdom of God. I feel that a lot of us want the Kingdom benefits, but we don't always want to serve God. We don't always want to get to know Him better, and even though the steps of the righteous are ordered by God, we don't want to seek Him out before we make major life decisions. If you are doing things like choosing a spouse and getting married without seeking God first, then you are setting yourself up for big trouble.

When you are in good standing with God, you will begin to realize how valuable you are, especially as He begins to release His blessings to you. Some of you reading right now were promised a lot of things from God. He hasn't forgotten His word. You don't have to remind him of His promises. You just need to get right with Him and stop delaying your blessings. Allow Him to show you the things inside of you that are hidden. Things you have not dealt with yet. Things you don't even realize have been sitting deep inside of you, just waiting for the right—or maybe, wrong time to manifest. Some of you, what's hidden inside of you are gifts or I like to call them, keys, to your prosperity. Could it be that the man you are trying to hold on to is the reason that you don't know what is inside of you?

The next question asked was whether or not you are looking to a man to save you. I can't tell how many times I have met a female who was waiting for a man to save her. Heck—at one point, I was that female. This is a thought and a way of thinking we've adapted early in life thanks to fairy tales, where the Princess is in a state of distress, and she is waiting for her prince to come along and rescue her. It is time we stop waiting for a man to save us. Instead, we need to start saving ourselves. I am speaking to the women who are financially unstable and think everything will be well—so long as you find your rich prince. Or to the woman carrying a lot of emotional baggage and you feel that it is the man's responsibility to fix you.

Look at your sons and look at yourself. Would you encourage your son to be with a woman who is guided by this frame of thought? Look at your daughters—maybe you don't have children yet; but is this the survival strategy you are giving her now to apply later on in life? If so, you are wrong. And you need to do something about that now. Sorry to shatter your fairytale, but prince charming is looking for a woman who compliments him. Meanwhile, you are asking God, *where is he*? Do you really think God is investing in one of his best men to then release him to a woman who is a mess and who isn't going to add to him? He needs you to get ready too. He needs you to get your life in order. Again, it starts with realizing that you need fixing. And it starts with turning over your mess to God and saying, God, I admit it, I need fixing. When you think that you are perfect, you leave no room to be fixed and you close the door in God's face. The truth is, we all have areas in our lives that need to be worked on. But if we are blind to those areas, we won't even take the steps necessary to ask God for help.

Let me say this as well. Just to clear the air: God can give you favor in a man's eyes, even in your mess. But that type of favor follows behind obedience. Once again, do you have a relationship with God, where you speak with him, where you seek him out daily, where you meditate on his word day and night? When you get to that place, heaven opens up for you, and nothing can stop you from getting the blessings that are in store for you. Nothing but you, anyway.

The next question I asked was whether or not you felt that you were at a place in life where you are emotionally healthy. I mentioned the importance of controlling your emotions in a previous chapter, and I'll bring it up again now. Some of you reading this may have a high intelligence quotient, but your emotional quotient is very low. Keying cars, pouring Clorox on clothing, setting flames to homes—none of these things are cute. While these actions may bring us a temporary and false sense of victory, you will find that you are still left with pain that needs soothing, wounds that need healing, and in some cases, criminal charges that follow you around for a lifetime. The best revenge is truly walking away in silence, working on a better expression of yourself as a woman, and then leaving the rest to God.

Waking up with Strangers

You cannot be so desperate to be loved by a man, that you are willing to settle for just any man. I get it, sometimes you just want to hear a deep voice on the other line, or to wake up in strong arms, even if they are strange arms. You want someone to check in on you after a long day and to simply ask if you are okay. That's an innate desire that we just cannot shake. What is not normal though, is doing so with a stranger who we know serves no role in the present chapter of our lives.

Here is where a lot of women go wrong too. We enter into relationships prematurely, meaning, we do so before we have a sense of self, and then when we start to learn more about who we are, we one day wake up next to a man who we no longer recognize. Then, we try to change them so that they become what we feel we need. That can't be right, can it? Now let's talk about this some more.

Starting off with the God factor once again. When you don't have a relationship with God, you are at risk of being misled and walking out of alignment with His true purpose. Some of you right now, are so derailed, you are working at a 9 to 5, when you know good and well that you are to be running your own business. Some of you are extremely wealthy, because of the gifts and natural abilities that are stored up inside of you, but you walk in poverty every day, because you are not in tune with yourself or with God spiritually. Here is what this leads to though: it ensures that you are always out of season and always struggling to make things work beyond the grace that you were given for those seasons.

We have got to stop waiting until after we have made the wrong decisions, to seek God. We need to be more proactive and not reactive. This is where you are losing time. If you are seeking God after the fact, you might find yourself in a position where God is saying to you, *that man that you have invited into your life, has to go*. Some of you, even when God speaks to you and gives you confirmation that the man you are with is not for you, you try to ignore God and force it to work. We force it by trying to change the man. Ask any male who has been in the position where a woman is trying to change him to be what she needs him to be, and see what he says. This creates resentment. It goes both ways. Has a man ever told you that you are not enough for him? You're not pretty enough, not skinny enough, thick enough, not light enough, not dark enough? These things push you away from a person instead of pulling you towards them.

Get Untangled From the Nets

You need to get out of all the nets that you are tangled in, or else you are going to drown right where you are. I find that one of the common instances where women often find themselves trying to change the man in is when she realizes that she is unequally yoked with him. If you are reading this and have found yourself in that situation, I encourage you to walk away, or to at least change the dynamics of your relationship, and pray that God illuminates the path for you for the new direction you are to go in.

Don't be so desperate to have a man, that even when you know that you will never accept him as he is, you still won't let go of him. I truly believe that there are some situations—very few—where if you let go and let God do what He has to do, that you will find that God will breathe life into that relationship at a later time. Of course, this is subjected to both you and that person's obedience. Now, don't let that last sentence give you any type of hope that something will work out. I am especially not speaking to women who are being abused. I am simply saying that, we cannot change people. We can only change ourselves. It is beautiful when two people in a relationship can evolve together. But when this does not happen, you have to build up the strength and self-control to move on. You need to accept who you are. You also need to accept who they are. Always be true to yourself.

Another net that women often find themselves tangled in, is a net where they are allowing a man to tell them who they are and who they are not. It is out of that desperate need to just be loved that we agree to be who someone wants us to be, and not who we are. I will never forget a date I went on in Atlanta—I'll explain what dating means to me later on in this chapter. But we went on a date, and I thought he was pretty cool. We were both practicing a vegan diet, we were both inspired by Egyptian teachings, and we both liked traveling. It was on our second date that I learned that he had self-esteem issues which were masked by a complex that suggested that women need to go back to their roles of just keeping their homes in order and raising children. I wouldn't be surprised if some of you agree with this, but please understand that we are now living in the age of the woman.

Women are rising up, they are coming together, and they are closing the gaps that they have been socialized to accept as normal. We don't want to live in boxes anymore. We are no longer psychologically committed to the archaic societal views on gender roles that say that we should get married and push out children by a certain age. Or that we should allow a man to control us, to the point he is abusive. We realize that we are a portal to life, through which humans enter into this world—and that alone makes us powerful. And still, we are so much more.

So there I was, sitting next to this guy after a dinner date and a long stroll through Centennial Olympic Park in Atlanta. Naturally, the question came up, of w*hat caused our last relationships to end.* I can't remember who threw the question out there, but he was answering it. He explained to me that he was no longer interested in his last girlfriend because she had too many aspirations and she wanted too much out of life. He was not interested in a woman who wanted to be great. He simply wanted a woman who wanted to be a wife to him and a mother to their children.

The warm air brushed past my face, carrying his words across the park with it. If he thought those things concerning a woman who simply wanted to open up her own clothing store, what was he going to think of me who had enough ideas that if someone gave me $10 million today, it would only take me a few days to put it to use and a matter of months to churn it into an empire.

I had a choice to make in that moment. I could've swallowed my dreams, smiled at him, and shrink myself small enough to appear as the perfect woman to him, or I could've scribbled down a mental note and told myself, this is not the man for you. I went with the latter. The date ended on a good note, but the next day, you best believe I told him how I felt, and why that meant that I was no longer interested in him. I am direct in that way.

Had I been desperate for a man, I probably would've kept on spending time with him and pursuing a relationship. The problem is, when we do this, women, we will realize later on in life that we have been living a lie. Suddenly, the man will seem like an enemy to us, when really, we have been an enemy to ourselves. This is why I say, it is not them. It is you. Stop entering into these relationships with no sense of self. Respect yourself enough to admit that you are not ready for what your heart is desiring. You are especially not ready when your heart is desiring one thing and something else is showing up in place of it.

Let's move on to the next activity. These questions are focused on one main question, which is, what is it that I really want? For each question, I want you to on a separate sheet of paper, write down the answers that come to mind.

1) What type of behaviors **won't** I accept in a man?
2) What things will I **not** compromise on in a relationship?
3) What areas of my life right now, should a man **not** have to deal with?

It is okay to not know exactly what you want in life. I feel that even though we may not know what we want, we somehow always have an idea of what we *don't* want. One way to do this is by dating with an open mind. Do it with the intention of getting to know someone and not necessarily dating to marry the first person who treats you to dinner. You have got to get better at interviewing these men too so that you can save yourself time. You will know you are good at this when it takes one conversation to know that a person is not for you. You don't even have to be creative with these questions, ladies. Some of these questions should be direct. *Do you drink? Oh, you do? Then I'm sorry. I'm not looking for that.*

See ladies, because of what I had gone through with my ex-husband, I was not interested in meeting a man who drank. At all! So that was one of my answers to the first question. I was also not going to compromise when it came to my relationship with God. This is something I would develop years after my divorce. I remember there was a time when I was not interested in a man who was Christian. Now that I am Christian, I am not interested in a man who does not know God. And in case you don't know this—there are a lot of people who carry the title Christian but still do not know who God is. There is nothing wrong with enlightening someone. Even better, is if you can find someone who enlightens you. Know yourself. Build a relationship with God, and don't rush into a relationship with someone just to be in a relationship. Finally, stop waking up with strangers.

Sorry, I am Under Construction.

To the last question, what areas of your life should a man not have to deal with? A lot of people will struggle to answer that question and the reason for this is because we are quick to point out the faults in other people, but we never really want to point out the faults in ourselves. I finally met a man who was worth introducing to the world. Who was worth marrying. Who I felt truly deserved someone better than me. He came at a time when I was under construction. I was not ready at all. And I was afraid to let him go and miss out on someone who I knew was truly amazing. Still, for some reason, I couldn't get excited about him, because I managed to allow myself to become so bitter over another situation that hadn't gone as I had planned. This particular person that I was bitter about, was not interested in me the way I thought he was. I had to come to terms with the fact that our friendship could not mature into a relationship, because that was not the person who God had in store for me. I had to accept the fact that he was honest enough to tell me that he didn't see us in a relationship.

But why was it so hard to believe this? Why hadn't I learned at that point in my life that it is okay for someone who I was dating to assess me and then make the determination that I was not the one? We cannot be so egotistical that we feel that a man does not have the right to choose who he wants to move forward with. Some of you ought to be happy that you were not chosen, because God truly had bigger and better plans for you. I am telling you, sometimes when a relationship ends, it is not them. It's you. Look at that statement both ways.

135

Some of you have things that you need to fix and until you fix them, they will turn away people from you. But also, I truly believe that God just won't allow any and any man to pick you. And I speak more about this in chapter seven, but I really want you to understand just how valuable you are to God, even in your mess. See, He knows the plans that He has for you and so He sees you walking in that light, and what He won't allow is for any man to interfere with His plan for your life. That is why some relationships will end abruptly. You won't know what happened. They won't know what happened. You just have to trust God.

The guy turned me down, and I was so hurt, I blocked him out of my life entirely, and I did it in that same hour. He couldn't call, text, email, iMessage, WhatsApp, Instagram, Facebook, the whole nine yards. But none of that was necessary. The guy had made his mind up. If anything, he was disappointed that we couldn't remain friends. We had, after all, dated with the understanding that we were simply getting to know each other and other people, in hopes that we could find someone to move forward with. That is truly my definition of dating. So, why did I diverge so far from something I believed in? Why didn't I have enough emotional intelligence to act more mature? I'm telling you ladies, we have to learn to accept rejection, especially when the man is being honest. He didn't drag me along. He didn't lie to me. He didn't mislead me. He wanted a woman. That woman was just not me.

I'll say this though, and I may lose some of my readers at this point. The reason why a lot of women struggle with rejection is because they have given away too much of themselves too early. Imagine I felt so hurt over being let down easily, even though we hadn't had sex. But imagine how much worse I would have felt if we did take it there? That's why it is so important to get to know a person before you take it there with them. Get to know their intentions. Do they want you or do they want a part of you? Not all men will be honest enough to say they don't want a relationship either. This is why it is important that you are dating with an opened mind and closed legs.

Don't Miss Out on God's Plan

Mr. Perfect showed up not long after I was turned down by this guy. I was so depressed, I hadn't even realized that what I was praying for had showed up. I was literally in a new transition in my life. I had just moved back to Atlanta for the second time, and not long after, was reconnected with someone I had met years before, and it never crossed my mind not one time, that this was a part of God's plan for me.

The beautiful part was that we were developing a close friendship where we were getting to know each other. Sometimes we would sit on the phone until the next morning, not a dull moment in between. We would go to dinner, or the movies, or for ice cream, and sit for hours after, just talking.

It wouldn't be long before he would ask me to consider taking our friendship to the next level, and it was at that time that I became defensive. *I don't want that*, I would tell myself. *But, girl you do!* There was a battle going on in my mind. I asked him to give me some time to think it through. And he did just that. He was very patient. We still spent time with each other, but I knew sooner or later that I would have to answer the question. The real problem I was having though is, I came to realize that I was asking God for something that I was not willing to sacrifice and prepare for. After a while, I found myself mistreating him. Speaking to him any old how. I was upset that he had showed up at a time when I just wanted to be miserable. I started cancelling dates and giving him excuses on why I couldn't see him and why I couldn't spend time with him. No matter how much I pushed him away, I realized that this man was still willing to be there for me. He still wanted to be a part of my life, even if it was not in the capacity of a relationship.

After I had succeeded in pushing him away, to the point where I told him I didn't want to see him at all anymore, I went back into a period of isolation. I hated myself for who I was becoming. I hated that I didn't want what I thought I wanted and what I had asked for.

I took a trip to Florida, and this was no leisure trip at all. I was retrieving some items I had left in storage some years ago, while I was overseas. Mr. Perfect was supposed to take that trip with me but because I had chased him away, I had to do it all alone. I removed the items from storage by myself and when I was done packing, I took the long nine-hour trip back from South Florida to Atlanta.

I wasn't completely alone though. God had taken that trip with me. He sat in that car with me, told me not to touch the music, not to turn on my Phil Hendrie Podcast, and not to take any phone calls. He and I were going to have a long conversation. And we did. He showed me that I was messing up big time. That I was about to let the enemy steal someone from me who was supposed to play a major role in my life. It was during that conversation that I realized that I had to make some immediate changes in my life and my attitude. If I was going to approach this man, he deserved the best version of me. It was right then and there that I decided to change.

It was a close friend of mine, Celeste, who I hadn't spoken to in months, who called me out of the blue and got me in my right mind. God couldn't have had her call me at a better time. In just minutes, I brought her up to speed on everything that was going on in my life. I will never forget what she said to me. "Are you crazy girl? You better get off this phone right now and go get your man!" So of course I swallowed my pride, I called him back, and I apologized for how I had behaved and how I had treated him. I didn't realize how much I had hurt him, but I explained to him that I needed the space to work on myself and to fully let go of some of the things I was holding on to. I let him know that nothing was wrong with him. The problem was me. I explained to him that I made the decision to change. My behavior was not a true reflection of who I really was. Not only that, but he deserved only the best part of me. I honestly did not want to miss out on someone that God had confirmed that He had sent into my life.

What part of your life do you need to change so that you can keep Mr. Perfect or Mr. Right or your Boaz, when he comes? No matter how patient that man was with me, if I had not made the decision to change my attitude, he would not have stayed with me, and rightfully so. I will never forget the night we spoke things over. He was very forgiving. Tears were rolling down my eyes as we spoke. I couldn't tell where the tingly feelings in my heart was coming from. I sat in the window and looked out at the same moon I had been mesmerized by, the night I slept at my granny's house. That night, I had written a prayer in my diary, asking God to bless me with a husband who loved me unconditionally. When I got off the phone with Mr. Perfect, I remember grabbing my diary, and scribbling the words, *Diary, I almost* chased away *my husband.*

Other People's Husbands

Speaking of husband, before I close this chapter, there is something that God wanted to make sure that I talked about. He wanted me to talk about other people's husbands. Globally, divorce rates have been on the rise, with over 50% of marriages heading to divorce, and subsequent marriages ending at an even higher rate. Among the many reasons why marriages end, infidelity and adultery have played a major role.

While I was preparing to write this chapter, it was dropped into my spirit that there are a lot of women praying for a husband to be released to them, pleading for a spouse and a partner that they can build with. The reason this hasn't been released to them, however, is because they are soul-tied to someone's husband. If this is you, you have an hour to release him!

I am not here to point fingers nor to condemn anyone. There was a point in my life, where the only type of men that came my way were married men. All of them with excuses—*oh, I am separated, oh, I did it for my documents, or I did it to help her.* Listen to me women, no matter what the excuse is, if you are looking for a husband, and the man who you are currently seeing is already married, you have a problem.

God is gravely vexed with many of his daughters concerning this matter and He is issuing a cease and desist order that says, *Let that woman's husband go*! Stop trying to prove to yourself that you are worthy, at the expense of someone else's marriage.

If you obey God's command and order in this hour, His promise is that He will bring healing to that area in your life where you are hurting, where you feel neglected, and where you feel unworthy. I shared this scripture in an earlier chapter, and I'll share it again. In 2 Chronicles 7:14 God's word says: "If my people, which are called by my name, shall humble themselves, and pray, and seek my face, and turn from their wicked ways; then will I hear from heaven, and will forgive their sin, and will heal their land." (KJV).

God loves you, woman of God; even in your sin. Even with the choices you have made. He knows who has hurt you in your past. He knows of the secrets you have kept hidden—even things that happened in your youth that got swept under the rug, that no one asked about or spoke about. He has seen your tears at night, when you cried yourself to sleep and desired to just be held and to be told that you were loved by someone. The beautiful part about God's love is that He is quick to forgive. He is also a God of restoration. I trust that you will walk away from that relationship and allow God to prepare you for what is yours. I am praying for you.

To the woman who was rejected

Dear woman of God,

You are suffering, not because of what happened, but because of *how* it happened. You were more than likely humiliated and whatever happened was so devastating, it left your enemies laughing and even some of your closest friends talking. You have been made a spectacle, but God is about to make you a spectacle all over again, because He is about to give you beauty for your ashes (Isaiah 61: 1-3). He will use your situation for His Glory and He is about to place you on a pedestal. In this season of your life God will allow you to see the downfall of those who despitefully used you and persecuted you.

When I learned that my ex-husband had re-married the woman whom I learned that He had been sleeping around with, I felt like insult was added to injury. Despite all He had put me through, I thought, well maybe the problem was me, after all! There was a war going on in my mind, day and night. I had no choice but to fight it. I had a company to run and a new life to build. I had no idea though, that God was going to allow me to come out strong. Woman of God, you are coming out of this one Strong!

145

About a year after we divorced and he remarried, I learned from a friend of his that the same things that I was going through with him, were some of the same things that the woman he had married was now dealing with. Woman of God, I want you to take your pen and paper and write: Revenge is Mine Sayeth the Lord! He was still drinking. He was still violent. It got so bad, he ended up getting arrested. I didn't rejoice at this news. I had gotten over him by then. I felt sorry for him and I was proud of her for doing what I didn't have the guts to do, which was to let him go to jail. Still I prayed for him. And I prayed for her. She needed healing too.

Woman of God, while you may feel that this is a time to rejoice over someone's downfall, I want to warn you that there is no room for that at this time in your life. It is important that you maintain your class and character. It is critical that you pray for those who have intentionally and unintentionally hurt you in the past. Also, pray for them as they begin to reap what they have sown. Pray for God's mercy.

As you begin to see the big picture, you will begin to thank God that He spared you the brunt of the storm. You will come out weeping for joy. You do not look like what you have been through and it is time for you to start looking like where you are going. When you put this book down, I want you to step forward in the new mind of your higher self.

In this next season of your life, People will begin to tell you that you look different, you speak different, you walk different. That's because the day you have been waiting on, is come. Say hello to the new you!

Sincerely,

Sileta

CHAPTER

6

THERE IS PURPOSE *in your pain*

WHEN PEOPLE HAVE THE POWER to disappoint you and to walk away from you, don't try to stop them. Let them go. A few years ago, I took a trip overseas to Barbados to attend a wedding wherein I was the maid of honor. I was ecstatic for my friend, and though I had never met the man, when she spoke of him, her eyes lit up, her words were sweet, and with each word she spoke concerning him, she was painting a colorful picture of the perfect man.

The evening before the wedding, I joined my friend, her family, and a few others who had taken long trips from different parts of the world to celebrate with her. She couldn't have chosen a more magical place. Even the ancient church with its tall arches and high ceilings was enchanting.

I managed to get some one-on-one time with the bride before practice commenced. She was beaming from ear to ear, her body was perfectly toned, and she was the most beautiful I had ever seen her. The moment was finally here! I couldn't wait to meet this special guy of hers. I had seen photos of him before and had tried to spot him when I arrived at the church, but he was nowhere in sight. When I asked for him, she told me that her fiancé was not on the island as yet and that he was flying in the morning of the wedding. My eyes spread to the size of two full moons as I gripped both of her arms. She calmed me down and told me that everything was going to be fine. It's just that there were issues with his flight. Her mom interrupted the conversation we were having when she called everyone to the front, instructing all of the bride's maids to line up outside of the church, paired with the groom's men.

We practiced our strides down the aisle, hand in hand, the flower-girl and ring-boy leading the way. Her fiancé's best friend, who was also his best man, was supposed to walk with me down the aisle. He was not on island either. Someone else filled in for him. We repeated our steps over and over until her mother was satisfied that we knew what to do. When practice was over, I kissed my friend on both cheeks. She assured me that everything was going to be okay and that I should go back to the hotel and get some rest. I took the quiet drive back to the hotel with a few others. None of us said a word. I went to bed that night with an uneasiness stirring up in my stomach.

Then the day came. The day we talked about as children. The day our mothers, our Sunday school teachers, and society had warned us that we should save ourselves for. I woke up early and was ready to be the life of the party, especially since as the maid of honor, my role was very important. I wanted to tease her with an early wedding present. It was a tantalizing piece of lingerie I had hand-picked for her in a luxury South Florida boutique. I placed a call to her to wake her up and to let her know I was on my way to her room, but before I could step foot out of the door, the sobbing on the other end of the line confirmed the sick feeling I was carrying in my stomach the night before. The wasn't on island. He wasn't going to show up. He didn't call to say he wasn't coming either. He didn't call at all that day.

Later that evening, I sat in silence next to her on the beach. The warm ocean breeze tossed our hair to and fro. The ocean playfully rose to our feet, then pulled back gracefully, like a kitten pouncing around and waiting for someone to play with it. There were no words to say to her that day. I had never been through something like this before. Sitting next to the ocean though, I realized that we were two small beings, existing next to something that was far greater than us. I realized that this thing called life was far bigger than anything she was feeling and anything I felt for her. She didn't say anything to me that day, but I knew she desired my presence. And so that was our routine for the next few days. When she finally spoke, she said to me, *"There must be a reason for this. There must be a purpose behind this pain."*

Turn it into a War Machine

It is so easy to get swept away in the pain of what happened to us, that we often allow ourselves to get lost in it, instead of being found in it. In chapter two, I gave you the word Catapult, and shared with you that the Latin version of the word means *war machine for throwing*. It is time you turned your pain into a war machine and to let it catapult you into something new. Use it, just like it has used you. Give it a purpose. Give it a name.

While I was working on this book, I stumbled across a young lady on YouTube who was telling her story about how she moved to Atlanta and not long after moving, met a man. Instinctively, she didn't want to connect with him, but did so anyway. It wouldn't be long after they met that they developed a relationship. Months after, on a routine visit to her doctor, she discovered that she had contracted HIV from this man. Not only that, but she would later learn that he knew that he was carrying the virus. In fact, he was actually born with it.

I was glued to my computer for the entire episode and couldn't believe that this woman had been brave enough to share her story with the world. God was faithful to her as well. She managed to get out of that relationship, where even with his condition, he was cheating on her. She managed to get away especially, from the mental abuse. When she left, God gave her a husband who loved her beyond anything that had happened to her. God gave her a beautiful family as well. What she did with her pain was she gave it a purpose. She didn't let the enemy come into her life, turn it upside down, and leave her there to die. She turned her pain into a war machine. Her story is not only saving women from walking in that same trap, it is showing women who were exactly where she was that there is life after tragedy. But we all have to make that choice of whether or not we are going to sit in our pain or allow God to re-purpose it.

You Were Rejected—And That's Okay

When I was a little girl attending grade school in Anguilla, we used to play sports or games on Thursdays. I still remember the pink T-shirt that said, Stoney Ground Primary School. Imprinted on the back of the shirt was a quote that said, "Together we Aspire, Together we Achieve." When Thursday mornings came, I always experienced two types of emotions, excitement to be out in the field and then the humiliation of being one of the last two people standing, hoping to be selected for a team. The truth is—I was not athletic, and even as children, the students knew that when it came down to sports, they couldn't take a chance with me. They had seen me perform. They knew my weakness. When I think back to it, sometimes the team leader was a friend that I shared snacks and lunch with. But it didn't matter. When we want to win. We choose winners.

When I look at some of the choices of men I have made in the past, I am forced to admit that I was never really selective. I didn't think of things like, how will this person add to my life? Will they make a great father one day? Will this man be a great role model to my son? What about my daughter? How will this choice affect the choices she make in choosing men? What type of behaviors will she grow to believe is normal or acceptable?

When I look back to situations that never matured into relationships, relationships that never matured—period, and then when I look at where I am presently, it makes sense now. None of those men could've matured to this chapter in my life. In fact, if I hadn't let go of those situations, I would not have met my Mr. Perfect—who ironically, is not perfect at all. But when I look at all that I have been through, and the happiness that I feel now, it was all worth it and it all makes sense. I was not selected for a lot of teams, but I somehow managed to score very high in the end.

Proceed With Caution

You need to know this, and you need to take heed to it: What you choose to do with your life and who you choose to share it with, will determine what the next twenty, thirty, and even the remainder of your life will look like.

Your best days are ahead of you, but you have to first understand how critical the choices you make in the next hour, day, week, month, and year of your life, are. Your suffering has been in your

155

sacrifice, and my word for you in this hour is that nothing you've been through has been wasted! God will use it all for his glory. When I realized that I was going to be a divorce statistic, I wanted to write a book to help women get through it. God spoke to me clearly and told me to put the pen and paper down. There was so much to learn, so much internalizing and conceptualizing. The smoke hadn't fully cleared yet, the outer bands hadn't passed. He knew that I was still going to wake up in the middle of the night sometimes and just cry. He knew that somedays I wouldn't want to talk to anyone. He knew that I wanted to take my frustration out on any man who tried to come into my life after that. I just was not ready to help anyone else at that time. Not with that energy, anyway.

A lot of you, in this hour, will start realizing what to do with what you went through. Some of you have stories sitting inside of you that God will begin to give you direction on how to write and release them. Some of you will receive instruction for opening new businesses, where you will be coaching and mentoring women. Non-profits will be birthed from some. A lot of you are already speaking at local organizations and meeting women around the globe, just because of what you have been through. You are learning that your pain was really tied to a greater purpose. This is why God is asking you to fully let go of what happened to you, to fully forgive so that you can completely tap into all that is due to you in this hour and season of your life.

Before we can identify the purpose in our pain, we must first find the purpose in our core existence. I have said this before, and I will say I again, if we do not know what we are here to accomplish, we will settle for who everyone else says that we are, and what they have to say about what we are to do with our lives. Your life is yours to live, and while you should seek advice from others, you must always seek God first. The thing is, you never want to step outside of his will. In Ephesians 5:17 (ESV), the word of the Lord says, "Therefore do not be foolish, but understand what the will of the Lord is."

Call God by His Name

One night, as I was spending time in prayer after a day of fasting, God asked me a question. He asked me did I know his name. The more I spend time in God's presence, the more I am realizing that when he asks me a question, he already knows the answer. But not only that, when he asks me a question, he expects me to seek him out for the answer. The following morning, I jumped on periscope and shared a live morning devotion with everyone who God sent my way. While I tried not to become distracted by comments, one man asked me if I knew who Yahweh was. I had heard it used several times, and I knew as much to know that it was a name for God, but I really didn't know anything about its origin. The guy commended me on my obedience to minister God's word. He also encouraged me to learn the names that God goes by and what they mean. I will quickly share two of those names with you and tell you how to use them.

Whatever tragedy you are facing in your life right now, I need you to know that God can turn it around for you. Not only that, but you should know that *Jehovah-Rapha* means the God that heals. Call out to him, and he will heal your pain. He can heal whatever sickness you are carrying in your body too. Sadly, a lot of our sins, especially sexual sins, expose us to diseases, that the enemy then uses to bar our blessings. These diseases can be both physical and spiritual. That is why some of you reading are suffering from infertility and other embarrassing diseases that have prevented you from having the confidence to find someone new. Some of you truly feel as though your lives have ended because of these things. I declare right now by the authority in me and by the power of God—Jehovah-Rapha, that you are healed. It is important that you start declaring and decreeing the same over your life and that situation right now too.

Some of you are battling with loneliness. It makes it hard for you to sleep at nights. Sometimes when you call your closest friends, they are nowhere to be found. When you start feeling lonely, instead of calling out to that friend of yours or to that man who has left you, call out to *Emmanuel*, which means, God is with us. He is waiting for you to say God, take me out of it. Call out to Him now.

Open Your Mouth—Break the Silence

I shared with you in the introduction, how the enemy tried to silence me and how he tried to rip the very tongue from my mouth. That was a spiritual revelation of how he was trying to prevent me from putting this book out there. The more he held me down in that encounter, the more I opened my mouth and began to cry out: "No Weapon Formed Against Me Shall Prosper!" If he tried to do it to me, he will try to do it to you too. Your voice is powerful, woman of God. You cannot afford to stay silent in this hour. It is time to open up your mouth and start declaring what the Lord has spoken over your life.

The enemy doesn't want to see you use your pain as a war machine to go forward. When you are commissioned by God to do a work, the enemy comes in like a flood. But Isiah 59:19 reminds us that when the enemy comes in like a flood, the Spirit of the Lord shall lift up a standard against him. As you are taking steps towards the work that God has called you to, you ought to know that God is with you, and all that has risen up against you, will soon fall. So, who does God say that you are, even in your pain and suffering? Very often, God will use the pain that we are facing to direct us back on the path that we need to be on. Sometimes, He has to allow our plans to be cancelled. Sometimes, He has to step in and uproot us to get our attention and to save us from further harm or damage. I truly believe that God knows best. He gives us free will, yes. And sometimes, he steps in to save us, because He loves you enough to want you to experience and inherit, all that He has in store for you.

Because we know there is purpose in your pain, what is He asking you to do that you have never done before? What is the enemy telling you that's not aligning with what God has shown you? Identify what the enemy is saying and shut it out of your mind. Turn down the volume from all the voices around you, maintain your composure, and take your first step towards God's orders. Maybe out of this pain, a ministry will be birthed. Perhaps from your hurt, you will start a healing program. It is because of what I went through that God was able to use me to help women around the world. He couldn't release me to do any of this though, until I stopped repeating the same cycles, until I understood what had happened to me, until I was completely healed from it, and until he could trust me to share my story from a peaceful place. So what exactly is God asking you to do with this mess?

Hearing God's Voice

I feel that a lot of us have continued to walk around blindly and confused, because we don't know how to hear God's voice. God speaks to us in a number of ways. He may send a stranger to walk up to you and confirm thoughts that were lingering on your mind for a while. For instance, a thought that says, maybe you should go back to that book that you've been writing and finish it up. While I was writing this book, he sent someone to say that to me. This is before I even knew that God had a plan for this book title, beyond what I had planned.

Some of you, God may have asked you to do something and you're not sure that you've heard from God, and so you haven't moved on it as yet. I declare that over the next few days, you will start to get the confirmation you need. Maybe when you jump in your car and turn on the radio, the first word out of the announcer's mouth, will be the exact thing that God has called you to do. This was a similar case with me, when it was impressed on my spirit that it was time to start my podcast ministry. I was hesitant at first, but then a number of recurring incidents kept happening, further confirming that I had been called to this task. Today, I host a show called The Cusp of Greatness Podcast on the anchor app, where I am an inspiration to listeners around the world. But why do we sometimes struggle to discern if it is God calling us to these things, or if it is something else? The reason I am asking you to learn to hear God's voice is because this will save you a lot of time, a lot of money, a lot of heart ache in the future.

When we spend time in God's presence, our ears are trained to hear his voice and our eyes are trained to see the things of God. This is why I said earlier and through the previous chapters that we ought to seek God first. When we don't seek him first, we end up in the wrong careers, we end up in the wrong relationships, we end up carrying our hearts in our hands when someone rips it out and hands it to us because they don't want it.

In Romans 8:30 he says, and those whom He predestined, He also called, and those whom He called, He also justified, and those whom He justified, He also glorified. When we spend time in God's word and in his presence, we begin to develop a relationship with him, and it is on that journey that he begins revealing his secrets and plans to us.

God tells us in this word, that his sheep know his voice, he knows them, and they also follow him. When we decide to follow God, we surrender to his will, allowing him to order our steps. That is why it is so important to know exactly who God says that we are. It is equally important to know what our purpose is. We were called before we were even formed in our mother's womb. The enemy knows this, and that is why some of you almost didn't make it to birth.

That pain that you are trying to heal from, it is important that you give it a deadline. It is important that you do not allow it to stop you from walking in your destiny. If you ever have the chance to do this, I want you to walk down to the ocean, sit or stand before it, look at how massive it is, how far it expands, and how much bigger than you it is. And then I want you to think of the plans that God has for your life, and then look at how small your current problem is, compared to what you are being called to. Don't allow this pain to pull you down. I am telling you, there is purpose in your pain. You will survive it. You will come out strong. And if you choose to, your story will be used for God's glory to bless, encourage, and save others.

The Call of God is Disruptive

When God calls us to a season, His call is often disruptive. His call may interrupt your own plans for your life in that particular season. Not to mention, His call may come at a time when what he is asking you to do may seem impossible. I need you to understand that when we are called by God, we are called according to His purpose and His grace. Whenever you answer the call of God, you are subject to transformation. And, when God is calling you to something, it often means that He is calling you away from something else. For some of you reading this, that something that He is calling you away from might very well be a toxic relationship or a relationship that He knows will not mature and go anywhere. God is all-knowing. He knows what that person has done to you. He saw you being walked all over. He saw you being trampled like a rose on the ground. He is telling you to get up, even with your brokenness, even though your petals have fallen off. Get up and go. He wants to make you whole.

The Rose in the Garden

I think back to my friend who spent her wedding day sitting in the sand, looking out at the playful ocean, on one of the most exotic islands in the Caribbean. How could a place so beautiful be branded with such a painful memory? I couldn't understand what would make a man treat her in that way. Where in all his love for her and her zest for him, did something get lost in translation? She was a Christian woman, raised in the church, and for all I know had never done anything displeasing in God's eyes. So what happened? This situation taught me a lot about life. It showed me that there is no such thing as a life without a challenge. We will experience ups and downs in some shape or form. Some of us might experience it in our relationship lives, meanwhile some of us might experience it in other areas. I do believe that we ought to learn from these challenges and I believe that we owe it to ourselves to find the beauty and the good in them.

It is important that you know that you are not what happened to you. You are made no less beautiful and no less worthy as a result of it. In William Shakespeare's play, Romeo and Juliet, there's a popular reference to a line that says, "A rose by any other name would smell as sweet". No matter what name has been attached to you, what statistic, and what title, all because of what you have been through, I need you to know that you are still that woman who God has called. You still carry that beautiful fragrance that reaches Him in your worship. He still considers you one of his best. One of the most beautiful roses in the garden. Yes, you may carry painful thorns, but you will still be the most sought-after flower. The best part is, God won't allow just any and any man to pick you from the garden. It is better to have been left at the altar than to have to stand in divorce court with a baby tugging at your dress, while you fight for custody and child support. We must always look for the beauty and the blessings in even the ugliest of situations.

It is Good that I was Afflicted

A lot of you will walk out of this season screaming, *it is good that I had been afflicted.* God will allow you to see what it is he was saving you from. He will allow you to see people who spat harsh words at you, turn around and eat their own vomit. Psalm 118:22 talks about the stone that the builder rejected and how it became the corner stone. When people see that you have survived the pain that they have inflicted upon you, it leaves them dumfounded and wondering how you made it through. Not only that, but they will begin to realize that it was God who took you through it. For those of you who feel that you are that rose that has been trampled on the ground, I want to ask you if you have ever heard about the rose that grew through the concrete. This is the season for you to push harder than you have ever pushed. It is the season that you will lean towards the sunlight and bloom into your true beauty. You are not too old, you are not too young, you are not too big, you are not too small, you are not too dark, you are not too light, you are beautiful just the way you are.

I will close this chapter with an activity. I want you to write out affirmations, prophetically speaking over yourself and where you expect to be in the next six to twelve months of your life. I believe that I AM affirmations are one of the most powerful activities you can ever do because we all have the power within us to prophecy over our own lives and to speak our way into the lives we desire. On the next page, I have shared with you several of my present affirmations, as a guide. Feel free to take from my list. I also encourage you to seek God out for direction on what exactly it is He is asking you to do. You don't want to miss the mark. You want to find out what God has for you. You want to declare it boldly and then you want to walk in full confidence knowing that you are doing just what He has called you to do.

I AM Affirmations

I AM every day, becoming more of the woman who God has called me to be. **I AM walking in full confidence, because I know that God is ordering my steps.**

I AM inspiring women all around the globe with this book and with my story.

I AM one of God's roses in the garden that no one can pick unless authorized to do so.

I AM bold. I AM beautiful. I am radiant. **I AM a virtuous woman. I AM a wife.** I AM making the enemy tremble, every day that I put my feet to the ground.

I AM not what happened to me but instead, everything that God says that I AM. I AM submitting my life to God's will and because of that, I am walking in full obedience.

I AM a powerhouse. I AM a force to be reckoned with. I AM the rose that grew from the concrete and the seed that bloomed into good fruit when the enemy tried to bury it.

PART three

For Such A Time As This

To the woman without a sense of purpose

Dear Woman of God,

I wrote a short story, maybe a year ago, but never published it. It was a story about three sisters who were very young, and how each one of them was introduced to womanhood in very abrupt ways. The first sister found out she was pregnant, and when she discovered such, she was forced into an arranged marriage. On the wedding day, with tears in her eyes, her mother kissed her and said, "You're a woman now."

The second sister learned that she was a woman when her menstrual cycle came down while she was sleeping soundly through the night. She was petrified at the sight of it. The blood had soaked the sheets and seeped into the mattress. She was only ten. As her mother prepared a bath for her the next morning, she smiled at her and said, "You are a woman now."

The third sister grew to be in her twenties and had never gotten an announcement that she was a woman. She thought that because of this, something was wrong with her. When she confronted her mother about it, her mother laughed and told her not to be silly, that

171

everything that she is and everything she ever will be, has always been inside of her, since the day she was born.

I thought about this story one day when I was speaking to my dad, and he shared with me that he was proud to see the woman I have become. He admitted that he had always known that I was destined for greatness. He always knew that it was in me and that is why he always wanted me to carry myself in a certain manner.

Well, I am sharing this with you because you too, like the third sister in my story, may be waiting for someone to tell you who you are. Maybe you are waiting for validation. The only validation you really need though, is the one that God gives you. He has planted somethings in you that He is getting ready to activate.

You're gonna need to change your wardrobe, because you are about to manifest into the woman he has called you to be. You are about to go further than any woman in your family, your hometown, or your country, has ever gone. I hear a stampede of women, rising up with you too. That means that you will be a woman of influence.

Your unique suffering is that you have been overlooked too many times and because of this, you have lost your sense of purpose. You have been waiting to be noticed. You have been waiting to be selected. You have been waiting, so much that your hope has been deferred. The bible says that hope deferred makes the heart sick (Proverbs 13:12). It then goes on to say though, that when that thing cometh, it is a tree of life.

God is saying to you, I will show you your purpose, and I will begin to show you in this hour. I don't know about you, but I am shouting as I write this letter, because I can see you in the spirit, and you are doing your thang! #SLAY

XOXO,

Sileta

CHAPTER

7

FOR SUCH A TIME *as this*.

ONE MORNING , while I was praising and worshipping God, he started speaking to me about some of the things he was getting ready to do in my life and the lives of some of the people around me. In the midst of that, he gave me an assignment. He was calling me into a deeper relationship with him so that I would know him on a deeper level. The first question he asked me was, do you know what a day means to me? This caught me off guard, because I couldn't understand what he meant by it and where he was going with that question. A lot of times we want God to give us the answers, but we don't realize that He wants us to seek Him out for the answer.

And so he led me to the book of Genesis, in the days of creation, where we see a breakdown of the magnificent things that God was able to do over the span of six days. On the first day, he created the heavens and the earth. He spoke light into existence, separating it from the darkness, and calling the light, day, and the darkness, night. This not only helped me to put into perspective just how majestic God is, but it taught me that a lot of us think we know God, but we don't really have an idea of what God is capable of and of what he can accomplish. It was on the fourth day that God created the stars and the heavenly bodies. The sun and the moon were among them. The movement of these bodies would help man to keep track of time. This amazed me, because not only did God create everything that is, He also created the element of time. This means that He is separate from time, and therefore not limited to it.

In 2 Peter 3:8, we are reminded that for God, one day, is like a thousand years, and a thousand years as one day. I believe that verse accomplishes a number of things, including demonstrating the frailty of man in comparison to an immortal God. It also opened my eyes to the fact that we serve a God who existed before time and will exist after time.

So then, my question to God was, well if you did such mighty things in one day, is there anything that you cannot accomplish in the space of an hour? We all know the answer to that question. Nothing is impossible for God. Not only that, but God is accelerating the healing of his daughters and He is stirring up the boldness that He has placed inside of them so that they may utilize it in this new season that has already been ushered in. You feel it. You know it. Some of you are overdue. And God is saying—I'm going to step into the natural and do something super, so that you can be emotionally ready for what I am getting ready to do in your life. Here's what a lot of us may not realize though. We fail to realize that when God is doing something in our lives, it is tied to a bigger purpose and it is all for His glory.

Moving along; so because mankind was placed into time, we are constantly limiting ourselves to it, to the point we dictate what we can and cannot accomplish, based on what we understand of it. Some might say that it is not healthy to try to get over a relationship in an hour. Meanwhile, I am saying to you, you have an hour to get over that relationship, and the reason for this is because this is the day that the Lord has made, and this is the hour that He wants to do a new thing in you. Not only that, but if you were truly honest with yourself, you would admit that the relationship was over, long before it even started. Because our mind is so powerful, it is constantly filling in the gaps for missing information, and very often, because we seldom live in the moment, a lot of details go overlooked.

How exactly are you perceiving your current situation? Has it consumed you so much that you have failed to realize that you are in an entirely new season in your life? Are you looking ahead to see all the great things that are in front of you or is your head turned backwards so that all you can see is that which is behind you?

I want to ask you to do something right where you are, right now, with this book in your hands. Cry out to God and ask him to deliver you from this stronghold, right now, so that you can move on to do the exploits that God is calling you to in this hour. This might mean that you have to accept an apology that was not given. It might mean that you have to realize that you messed up or that they messed up, but that there is nothing you can do about that now, except to keep moving on. You have to forgive yourself and forgive them.

It was on the sixth day that God created man. This made me wonder why he had created man on that day. Then it made sense that He hadn't just placed man into space, without a designated place and without the element of time. Instead, He first created all the things that man would need, and then on the sixth day, placed man into His habitat. I want you to follow with me closely, because some of you may be wondering, well where is she going with this.

The Making of Eve

God didn't place man on the earth without giving Him instructions. First, He showed man that every animal had a companion and that man was without one. From this, He determined that it was not good for man to be alone. And so He gave woman onto man. God gave man a helper who was fit for him. It is important that you understand this because a lot of us women have the wrong idea about men and the role they are to play in our lives. Not just that, but too many of us overlook the word helpmate and feel that this means that we should bring nothing to the table.

You have to bring more than your beauty, your body, and definitely more than sex to the table. Any man who is a real man, will demand more than those things out of you. He will want you to have goals. Not only that, but he will realize the role that he is to play in enabling and supporting you through those goals. Don't get it twisted either. It goes both ways. Help-mate means that you are helping someone who has something going on that you are now adding to. Remember, Eve was added onto man.

Lord, What is my Purpose?

It is very possible that you have come to the end of your relationship and suddenly you feel as though you have no identity. You may be asking yourself, *what is my purpose?* When that question is raised, it means that you are right where you need to be. It means that you are discovering you. This is one of the indirect results of pain. It forces us to react to it. It forces us to deal with it. Some of the best music, art, stories, books, movies, have all been conceived behind some level of pain or trauma. What are you about to create as a result of your pain?

The Stages of Grieving

It is natural to grieve for something you feel that you have lost. Elisabeth Kübler-Ross, a Swiss-American psychiatrist, wrote a groundbreaking book called *On Death and Dying* where she first introduced her theory of the five stages of grief. In the first step, which she labeled as denial, she explained that the world becomes meaningless and it makes no sense. This step usually puts us in a state of shock. When the last straw was pulled in my marriage and everything came tumbling down, an unusual peace had fallen over me in the days following. Still, even though a peace had fallen over me, for nearly a month, I was in shock.

Some days, I found myself reliving the pain I endured in the relationship, all over again. When I learned that he had married to the same woman he was cheating with, that was a hard blow to my stomach. Even then, I was in denial. I couldn't believe that this had happened to me. It sounded like it could have been anyone's story, but not mine.

When you have gone through your denial phase, you may start to experience some anger. Anger is a natural emotion. It is okay to feel angry, especially when you realize that you've sacrificed so much of who you are for someone else. Especially when you've given 100 to them and they only showed up with 25. Some of you may feel angry because they were supposed to be there for you and your children. Now instead, they have neglected you and have started a family with someone else.

I have to admit, sometimes my anger was towards myself. I blamed myself for staying. I had other reasons to leave. I should've left because he was abusive. I should've left because of the alcohol. Those should've been my breaking points. Why did it take infidelity to make me leave? At some points, I was angry with him. He was supposed to be there for me. He was supposed to love and protect me. So when did he become the person that I needed to be protected from?

At times I was angry at the other woman too. I wanted to know what type of woman could feel secure in knowing that she tore apart a marriage. I felt like she knew too much about me and that she played a huge role in inflicting some of my pain. That was too much power for any woman to have over me. Of course, our anger should never be directed towards the other woman, but it was what I felt in that moment. And I know I am not alone in this. It is what a lot of my readers are feeling now or may have felt at some point.

This emotion is not necessarily unhealthy. It is something that manifests on our journey to healing. We think through stuff. We sift through the uncomfortable feelings. We experience fear. We wonder what these new discoveries will now mean for us. For a lot of women, the fear is whether or not they will be able to provide for themselves and for their children, now that the man is no longer in the picture. Maybe the man left or maybe you left. It still shakes our world up. Anger is not unhealthy, unless of course, you don't know how to manage it.

It is very important that we as women learn how to channel our anger when dealing with a deceitful or abusive partner, or any situation that leads to a breakup. Anger becomes unhealthy when we make others suffer for what we are feeling. It is not right to take that anger and frustration out on your children. It is not right to bring that anger into the workplace. Or to throw it on complete strangers. You have to work on your emotional intelligence and master it to the point where you have the capacity to take control of yourself and to express your emotions in a healthy way.

For me, poetry became that healthy medium of internalizing what it was that I was feeling. It was something I always loved doing as a child and was re-introduced to in my early twenties. A friend of mine, nick-named, *Rock Star*, contacted me one day just to check in and see how I was doing. I was not doing too well at all. Even though other areas of my life had started flourishing, I had been sitting in my anger, so much that it isolated me from the real world. When he picked up in my voice that I wasn't doing too well, he started laughing and said to me, "Are you in your right mind? Do you realize that this divorce—separation—whatever it is—could be the best thing that has ever happened to you?"

I hadn't seen it that way. Even though I knew that I hadn't really lost anything. Still, the enemy within me was trying to trick my mind into thinking otherwise. I suspect that this is what the enemy has been doing to you as well. Rock Star went on to make a suggestion. He didn't give me time to say yes or no. He suggested that I put my pain to paper and make something beautiful out of it. He went on to invite me to poetry that night and I agreed. I met him at a small hole-in-the-wall poetry spot with a sheet of paper in my hand.

I dragged that pain to the stage, the paper shaking in one hand, the mic in the next, the only strength left in me came through my voice, and I let it out. It was the sweetest remedy for something so tragic. I lost a husband, but I found two new loves. I found God and I found poetry.

There was a time before the divorce when my husband came back and wanted us to work things out. I had gone through tremendous growth at that point. I wanted to believe that he had changed. I wanted to believe that he had stopped drinking. I wanted to believe that he wouldn't hurt me anymore. I wanted to believe that this woman wasn't in the picture at all. I was now going through the bargaining stage of grief. I wasn't bargaining with my husband though. I was bargaining with God. I wanted Him to allow me to go back. Then I thought of my new-found love for poetry. I was performing several nights per week at different locations, and I was not just finding healing for myself, but others were being touched by my words. And so going back to this man would've meant that I was going to put away the new Sileta that I had found. There was no way he was going to be comfortable with me going out there to speak about things that I had been through with him. He wasn't mature enough for that. But it also wasn't God's will that I returned to Him. I knew that it wasn't God's will because God was already showing me parts of is His vision for me. Where poetry was concerned, He started showing me what He was going to have me to do with that pain. He was going to use me to change lives. He put words in me that He was going to allow to reach other women so that they could find their healing.

After the divorce, I felt guilty. I was thinking, *well—maybe it was my fault*. Maybe I made him into the person he had become. Perhaps if I had been softer, he would've treated me differently. I felt that I had given up on my marriage and should have fought for it. This is the mentality I had taken on, even with the growth I had achieved. The next stage of grief after guilt is depression. At this point I had moved to Georgia, but I still felt out of place. God sent me into complete isolation. It was in that time though, that I was able to hear his voice more clearly than ever before. That was my discovery point. I spent time getting to know myself. I started discovering who Sileta was.

The singer, Sade, has a song called *The Big Unknown*, where she talks about going back to a place where there was a wreck, and in that song, she realizes that she needs to go back and pull herself from the wreck so that she could save herself. That's exactly what I was doing. I was pulling Sileta from the wreck, wiping her off, stitching the wounds and then promising her that I would never allow her to get to a place like that ever again. What type of promises do you have to make to yourself right now? What is it that you owe to yourself? Maybe it is time to pull yourself from the wreck.

The final stage of grieving is acceptance. I remember walking through my apartment one day, and it was clear to me—I was divorced. It was God's will. The man didn't deserve me. The woman did me a favor. I had survived the wreck. I was well. I was no longer working two jobs just to sustain. God had given me a business of my own. My business was flourishing. I was able to take care of myself without having to step foot outside of my apartment. God was good to me. I had finally come into a stage of acceptance. Nothing I had been through was going to be wasted either. With this book as a witness, God turns it all around for His glory.

Give a Shout of Praise!

I encourage you to put this book down right now and give God a shout of praise. He can do for you what He has done for me. The very first step though, is obedience. If He tells you to pack it up and move to an entirely new city, would you do it? He is telling you that He is going to provide for you and your children once you leave that man, but do you believe? You have to remember that God is a provider. It is not the man who has been providing for you up until this point. It is God. It is not your job that has been providing for you either. God always takes care of His children. If you are believing all that God is saying to you in this hour, I want you to start giving Him a shout of praise, because God's word will not fall to the ground.

To the woman with the counterfeit man

Dear Woman of God,

While I was working on this book, I received a vision where while I was at home, I looked up to the sky and saw an angel in the clouds and it was carrying a basket. This created excitement in the atmosphere as spectators gathered around to see something they had never witnessed. Once the angel made it to ground level, the basket was now a garden tub and it was filled with gifts, which I understood were the answers to prayers that had been sent up by several people. I remember peeping over the shoulders of two spectators and I watched as the angel pulled gifts from the tub and started handing them over; one of those gifts being a newborn baby that was passed to a proud mother.

I looked on in amazement as the people received the answers to their prayers. After the angel passed out the gifts, it called my name and it called my grandmother's name. The crowd parted as we both stepped forward. I was a bit confused as to why I was being called, especially since there were no gifts left in the tub. But then the angel said, sit in the tub. I followed the orders and my grandmother followed too. Once we were seated in the tub, it was filled with milk and honey that flowed from the heavens. Then the angel said to me, "*Drink of it and bathe in it. This is your season of milk and honey.*"

I share this vision with you because this is the season where you too will receive breakthrough in your life. You have been praying through the night hour and have wondered if the morning of joy will ever come. You have suffered long, and hope deferred has made your heart sick, but God is about to turn things around for you and He is about to bring you into the land of milk and honey. The coming chapter was written to offer you hope so that you won't throw in the towel. So that you won't miss this new season. There is an angel tap-dancing on the clouds above you who is about to deliver the promises of God to you.

Still, even though you are so close to your blessing, you have a problem. Your unique suffering, God has revealed to me, is that you are conflicted by old things. Some of these things, you haven't realized that God has already healed you from. These are things from the past. Words that were spoken over you. Wounds that failed relationships have opened. I see in the spirit that some of you have been introduced to men who God has already strategically placed in your lives to be your husbands, but you are self-sabotaging the relationship because the doors to your past are still swinging open. Listen to me and hear me clearly—your past is the past for a reason. Say goodbye to those people who walked away when you needed them the most. Stop giving people access to your life who only see value in you when someone else has expressed interest in you.

Everything you've been through in the past few months and years have led up to this moment and I want you to put on the spirit of anticipation. Get rid of the Mr. Wrong and move forward with Mr. Right.

God's blessings be with you!

CHAPTER

8

A SEASON OF *Milk and Honey*

Mr. **PERFECT AND I** traveled to New York City one winter with another couple. It was his birthday, and he had never been to New York City before. I was excited to be a part of this first-time journey with him, especially since my earliest days in the United States were spent in the concrete jungle. Funny enough, I spent four years living in New York City and didn't know much about the city at all. I had no clue how to catch the trains or buses, and I relied on Mr. Perfect to lead the way, as I was constantly getting us lost and setting us behind schedule because of it. One of the places I was excited about taking him to was a small neighborhood in Manhattan called Washington Heights where I completed my first two years of high school. He was also going to be meeting my father for the first time, and so we were both looking forward to that. I should also mention that on that trip, I was anticipating nothing more than having him try a slice of New York-style pizza from a hole in the wall pizza spot outside of the 191st train station. Sure, Atlanta has good pizza, but nothing ever really beats the real deal, right?

Other than trying to pad the biting cold with our winter coats and me not being able to walk in 6-inch over-the-knee boots, the trip was splendid. Mr. Perfect got the opportunity to see the world-famous Time Square with all the lights and life teeming through it. He was also able to catch a glimpse of the subway musicians—some of the best talent in the world by the way.

The part of the trip that we still laugh over to this day though, was how a Chinese lady sold us two pairs of gloves and hats in the winter—proclaiming that they were the true UGG brand. We didn't need much convincing either. We were cold. The price was right. He pulled out his wallet and paid her in cash. She thanked us both, and in no time, disappeared in the crowd on the sidewalk. As quickly as I could, I slipped my fingers into the gloves. They looked like the real deal indeed. That was, until, a gust of wind blew and with it went the letter "G" from one of my gloves. We stood looking at each other for a moment before exploding in laughter.

"Welcome to New York, Babe," I told him.

But it made me think. How many times in life do we fall for the counterfeit, even when we know it is not the real deal? Sometimes the counterfeit looks so much like the real deal, we ignore all the red flags that say otherwise. It always seems to come at a time when we are most desperate too. The woman caught us while we were in the cold. It was right at the tip of our mouths, that we needed gloves and hats, and there she was! Sure the gloves kept us warm and the entire situation made us laugh. But when it comes down to real life, where hats and gloves represent the people who we are inviting into our lives, we can't take the same chances. This is why it is important that we check people out before saying yes to them. Don't be afraid to ask questions that are uncomfortable. Listen with more than your ears, so that you can discern just how genuine these people are.

Don't be afraid to ask a man what his plans are for you, and more importantly, ask him what his plans are for his own life. If he doesn't have a plan for himself, then you best believe, he doesn't have a plan for you. One thing with counterfeits, they can only fake for so long before they disappear into the crowd, and when they disappear, they often leave with something that is valuable to you.

Don't Pour New Wine Into Old Bottles

The fastest way to mess up something new is to contaminate it with something old. Think of what happens when new wine is poured into old wineskins. The wine seeps in and bursts the skins. Mark 2:22 teaches that new wine is for fresh wineskins. Still, a lot of women, after having survived breakups, after having made tremendous growth, after being molded into entirely new people, they go backwards and invite old things to part take into new things.

Could it be that you cannot move forward with the man who is God's perfect will for you, because you are still taking phone calls from someone from your past, you are still meeting with them in private, you have even continued to share your body with them? If so, these things are only further separating you from God and they are also standing in the way of your win in this season.

It is possible too, that you may have moved on a long time ago but have not been transformed by the renewing of your mind, and so out of habit, you are still entertaining your past? Some of my readers will know exactly what I am talking about. You have adapted the mindset that it is best to entertain something old, while you are getting to know someone new; this way, you have a backup in case it doesn't work. If this is you, you have to cut this behavior out right now, because you are about to chase away someone who God has sent or is sending into your life. You are about to turn someone away from you, right as they might be considering marriage. You are about to give someone reason to have second thoughts concerning you and the type of person that you are, all because you have allowed the enemy within you to deceive you.

Of all the chapters in this book, you are the woman who is closest to receiving the blessing of a new relationship, a new marriage, a new family. Can you afford to miss out? Is that not what you have been asking God for? You are close to going into the land of milk and honey, and you might find that the enemy is distracting you in this season, because he wants to blur your vision and show you other choices that are out there, in hopes that you will miss out on the perfect will of God. Can you afford that?

Let Unfinished Business be Unfinished Business

Have you ever noticed that while you were not seeing someone, no one called you, no one noticed you, no one showed interest? But the moment you've met someone new, suddenly, you are the most attractive woman. Suddenly, you're in demand. All of a sudden, men from your past, men you've never met, and men from every corner are suddenly attracted to you? You need to learn to smile, say good morning, good afternoon, good evening, and keep it moving. For the person in your past who is suddenly reaching out to you, texting you, calling you, it is time you inform them that *that* chapter of your life is over. It would probably be best if you don't even respond at all. If they didn't want you when you were a caterpillar, then they don't deserve you now that you have morphed into a beautiful butterfly.

It is easy to be tempted to entertain someone from your past because you may feel that you have unfinished business. These are some of the soul ties I spoke about in the second chapter. Sometimes when you think you have broken those ties, and you are about to start something beautiful, the enemy will test you. This is why you need to let unfinished business be just that—unfinished business. The reason it was unfinished in the first place, is because that person decided to start something with someone else or they didn't think you were good enough to pursue. Not everyone deserves access to the new and evolved you. Some of these people, you need to cut them, their friends, and their family off.

I recall being contacted by someone from my past, while I was dating Mr. Perfect. This wasn't even someone I had a relationship with. We were at one point, very much infatuated with one another. Well, the individual, who was also seeing what he might call his Mrs. Perfect, or the woman of his dreams, reached out to me and was curious to know how serious things were between Mr. Perfect and I. I explained that it was very serious, to the point that we have already started talking about marriage. After hearing that, he went on and made the proposal to me that we both should take a vacation to somewhere exotic and be with one another, before we both moved on to new marriages.

I analyzed the message for weeks. Not because it was something that I wanted to consider; but it made me think of how we as humans can get so close to something we have always dreamed of, and with one bad decision, we can risk losing it, for one selfish moment. We have to know the value of what we have so that we are not quick to jump when random proposals and offers come our way. And in case you are wondering, I declined the silly getaway. Not only that, but the audacity of him to think that he could approach me in that way? Furthermore, there was no way I was going to allow anyone on the outside to interfere with the beautiful love story that I had been blessed to find myself playing one of the lead roles in.

The Bird in Your Hand

When you have a lot of options coming your way, it is easy to forget what exactly it is that you have in your hand. You begin to second guess it. You wonder if you could've made a better pick. You begin to get a little *big-headed* and because you realize that you are the best thing since sliced-bread—*because some of us really are*—you feel that you need to let go of what you have. A lot of women and of course men, have been deceived in this way. They let go of what was once the dream, only to give themselves to their worst nightmare. Do not let greed prevent you from walking into your season of milk and honey.

The devil is a master of the counterfeit blessing. That's when he sends a man your way, right before he who is supposed to show up does. Or, he sends someone to make you question what is in your hand. That person would normally show up with everything that your guy doesn't have. He might be a little taller than the person you're with now—even though your guy is tall. Or, even though your guy may be well off, this one will show up with a lot more money. And he might even be more handsome. Sounds good, right? And then not even a year later, you start to learn what's wrong with him. He has a temper. He is controlling. He has a wife. He beats her. He's beating you. And the list goes on.

Go on a Fast

I shared in the opening letter of this chapter, how I saw an angel come down from the clouds and how the angel poured milk and honey over my head and my grandmother's head. While I was writing this chapter, I was reminded of a similar vision that I had, where I didn't see an angel, but I saw objects in the sky that were in transit to me. I saw a house, I saw the vehicle I had been praying for, and a few other things. God wanted me to see that my prayers were already answered so that I wouldn't get weary in waiting.

When the vision was over, I was pressed down by maybe seven demonic spirits. While I could not see them, I could hear them speaking, from where I was laying across my bed. One of them, who I'm guessing the leader, spoke to me and told me that everything that was coming to me, he could get them to me sooner than God could. He reasoned that all I needed to do was to agree with him that I would choose to receive it from him instead. So he wanted an agreement from me. I couldn't open my mouth at that point to chase him away or even to pray. But thank God the Holy Spirit intervenes on our behalf. Eventually, the spirits left, and I was able to get up and start praying. At that point, I did not have a strong prayer life, but God still allowed me to see things that were happening in the spirit realm.

I need you to understand this: Anything that the devil is offering to you in place of what God has for you, will always be a counterfeit and his goal will always be to rob you of your true blessings. The bible tells us that enemy prowls around like a roaring lion, seeking for someone to devour (1 Peter 5:8). That is why we need to be vigilant and conscious of what is happening in our atmosphere at all times. The enemy's plan is to kill you, steal from you, and to destroy you. But not in this hour, because now you are wiser.

Some of you need to go on a fast for the next 3, 7, or even 21 days so that you can draw closer to God and so that you can be protected under his covering. The fast gives you the strength you will need to be able to step into the spiritual realm and command the areas in your life where you have lost control, to align in divine order. Declare that thine will be done in earth as it is in heaven. Some of you already have the things you are praying for in the spirit, and you need to speak life into those things so that they manifest. I sense deeply that a lot of my readers will not only be praying for material things or to get rid of emotional pain, but a lot of you need healing—in your physical bodies. Speak over your life and declare your healing!

There is a war going on in the spirit realm to block the blessings that are coming your way. It is no wonder that some of you are being distracted with the counterfeit blessing. In Daniel 10, we learn of how Daniel had been praying and fasting for 21 days. When the angel arrived, he explained to Daniel that his prayers had been answered the moment he uttered them but the reason the angel was only now showing up was because he had to fight with the fallen angels in the third heaven. God had to send the warring angels to respond to Daniel's prayer.

Some of you reading right now have been praying and you have been fasting. You have been asking God for a breakthrough. You have been wondering if God has even heard your prayers. He has heard you. He will answer your prayers. Do not grow weary in well-doing. Do not give in to the enemy. Do not settle for the counterfeit. An angel is in the clouds and it is about to deliver your answer.

The Voices in Your Relationship

One of the worst things that you can ever do in a relationship is let too many voices in. As women, we do that a lot. We tell our friends everything, and then get offended when everyone has something to say about the men in our lives. We put our business out on Facebook or on social media and expect people not to have a say or to react to it. I encourage you that when you've found someone worth keeping, protect that person. A lot of you may not realize it, but the moment you open up and start telling some people that you found love, no matter how much they know that you deserve it, no matter how much they have seen you suffer in previous relationships, if they themselves are not happy where they are, they will try to ruin what you have going on. You have to know who these people are, and you have to learn to keep your mouth shut around them. Keep your man to yourself, for a very long time, before sharing him with the rest of the world.

Another thing a lot of us fail to realize is that none of us are perfect, and so the first minor thing our partner does that upsets us, we run and tell. Sometimes you have to allow yourself to internalize it first so you can determine how you really feel about what happened and whether or not you've overreacted or under-reacted. Do that before you pick up the phone and start calling all of your girlfriends about it. Invite God into that conversation that you are having with yourself as well. Some of the things that happen in your relationship should never make it outside of your relationship. Period.

You have to learn to protect your partner and to be a friend to your partner as well. That means, you don't need to run and tell your friends the personal and sometimes embarrassing things that he has confided in you with. I am telling you from experience, not all of your friends have good advice to offer you. Some of them have never even been in a relationship. Some of them don't even like you. I really need you to let that sink in, because I sincerely feel that a lot of women have lost good men because they have allowed too many voices into their relationships. If this is you, it is time you shut those voices out and start taking your business to God. Let him direct you from there.

I want you to remember this as well, just as your partner has flaws, so do you.

Time is of the Essence

Writing is something that has always come easily to me. I have always bragged about being able to whip out several chapters in a day or a manuscript in a week. This book though, has been one of the most challenging things I have ever written. It forced me to re-live periods of my life that I did not want to journey to. It forced me to re-live pain that I didn't have the tolerance to bear. It even forced me to cry for the first time, over things that I never took the time to mourn over.

I fought with God over this book. I was upset that He had chosen me to write it. I was upset that because I said yes to writing it, the enemy came in like a flood to attack me in many areas of my life. Towards the end of writing this book, my own relationship came under attack, and I remember laughing to myself and saying, *well, you are the author of Get Over Him in an Hour*.

One of the questions I started asking myself during this time was whether or not there is such a thing as "The One". I will say yes. There is such a thing as The One. But when we ask that question, we seldom ask it concerning our own choice of a mate. Instead, we ask this question because we want to know if the person we are seeing is the one, in God's eyes. Many times though, we are the ones rejecting the blessings that God has sent our way. *He's too short. He's too dark. He's too light. He doesn't have the type of money I expected my future husband to have*. I know of a family member who only dates men who drive a certain type of car—the foolishness! Many of us as women, are guilty of thinking this way too, but then we allow ourselves to be swayed by men who put their hands on us. Men who sleep around on us. Men who put us last. If you know without a doubt that you have a good man in your life, yet you are running from him because he is not your usual type, I am begging you to seek God for direction before you sabotage what might be the biggest blessing He has sent your way.

When we ask God to bless us, we sometimes fail to realize that he sends these blessings through the people we are connected to. A blessing might come in the form of a word being released over your life. It may come from a stranger who bumped into you at the coffee shop. It may even come to you in the form of the man you've criticized because he's too short, too dark, too light. I am not telling you to settle. No, not at all. I am suggesting though, that when true love finally shows up on your door, when the angel shows up with your milk and honey, that you will have the wisdom to at least recognize it. Finally, when a situation has reached the end of its season, bow out gracefully and, well—get over it. Time is of the essence.

Other Books by Sileta

Think Outside Your Cubicle is a personal account of Hodge's journey from the workplace towards entrepreneurship. Within these pages she is literally an open book, touching on some of the embarrassing mistakes she made early on in her career as a freelance writer and as a business consultant. It is a quick read but by the time you've turned the last page, you will be empowered and fueled with a new-found passion for business.

About Sileta

Sileta Hodge's personal experiences in marriage, relationships, and her Christian Faith, has played a role in informing her writing. As Founder of *Women With Diaries*, a literary movement bringing women together from all corners of the globe, Hodge has become a catalyst for change and an international voice of hope. Outside of writing, she publishes inspirational messages on her weekly podcast, *The Cusp of Greatness Podcast*. A future marriage and family-therapist, it is her goal to continue her legacy in healing families, one woman, one man, one child at a time. An island-girl at-heart, Hodge draws much inspiration from traveling to the Caribbean islands of Anguilla and Nevis.

Stay in Touch

SILETABLU.COM

Made in the USA
Columbia, SC
30 November 2019